WIT & WISDOM OF
KINGS &
QUEENS

WIT & WISDOM OF
KINGS &
QUEENS

MARIA PRITCHARD

CONTENTS

6   INTRODUCTION

12   ANCIENT ACUMEN

26   MEDIEVAL MONARCHS AND RENAISSANCE RULERS

36   MONARCHY IN A MUDDLE

54   QUICK-WITTED QUEENS

76   THE AXEMAN COMETH... AND OTHER DYING WORDS

86   MONARCHS BEHAVING BADLY

98   MODERN MONARCHS

112   THE HOUSE OF WINDSOR

136   THE PRINCE OF GAFFES

146   THE REST ON ROYALTY

INTRODUCTION

Until the 19th century, monarchy was the most common form of government throughout the world. Today, however, few nations have retained their monarchies and the majority of those that remain are constitutional. This means that the monarch exercises a mainly ceremonial role but has little or no political power. Only around 44 nations still have a royal head of state and of these, 16 are members of the same Commonwealth, headed by Queen Elizabeth II.

Although time has seen a reduction in the number of sovereigns, as well as a diminishment of their power, some countries have bucked the trend and re-established their monarchy in the 20th century. In 1975, Spain brought back their royal family after decades of dictatorship came to an end. King Juan Carlos had been named as the next head of state by dictator, General Franco but the King quickly set about introducing democratic reforms to the country. The Spanish Constitution was approved by referendum in 1978, establishing a constitutional monarchy.

Denmark has one of the oldest, continual monarchies, stretching back more than 1,000 years to the Vikings. The current Queen can boast the likes of Gorm the Old (d. 958), Harald Bluetooth (d.987) and Sweyn Forkbeard (d.1014) as her ancestors. Norway also has a continuous royal line reaching back more than 1,000 years, to Harald Fairhair, who became king in 872.

The Imperial House of Japan is the oldest continual hereditary monarchy in the world, generally considered to begin with the surprisingly long-lived Emperor Jimmu (c. 711–585 BC). The current Emperor Akihito (1933–) is considered to be a symbolic head of the people and his role is purely ceremonial. By contrast, Holland has one of the newest kingdoms: it was established in 1815, with its royal members supplied from the House of Orange-Nassau. Their power is limited and the monarch remains politically neutral.

Most contemporary royal houses are fairly pared down in size, making them less of a drain on the public purse. The absolutist Saudi Arabian family are an exception: they are a vast family, numbering several thousand over six branches. All the members are paid a stipend and the more significant figures inhabit the positions of authority in government – but only the males, of course.

In most cases, the traditional roles of the monarch have long been eroded. Few make their nation's laws and fewer still would lead their countrymen into battle. However, occasionally their role as figurehead can still play an important part in their nation's well-being. During World War II, the actions and attitudes of some European royals helped to encourage their subjects' defiance. The British royal family remained in London, even during periods of heavy aerial bombing and their palace suffered direct hits. This act of solidarity helped to focus a sense of unity among the British but was also a gesture which had a lasting, positive effect on the nation's attitude towards the family. Similarly, in Norway, King Haakon's refusal to surrender to the Nazis helped to rally Norwegian resistance. He used all of his influence to persuade the government not to co-operate with the invaders and it worked. King Haakon, Crown Prince Olav and the cabinet ministers were forced out of the capital and eventually evacuated to the United Kingdom by British forces. From this exile, they regularly broadcast inspiring messages back to Norway.

Although monarchy may seem an anachronistic institution, with little of relevance to our contemporary world, interest in royalty appears undiminished. Their exploits and fashion choices seem to claim more column inches from the world's press than ever before. Glamorous, well-dressed royals can bring invaluable media attention for worthy causes. Pictures of Princess Diana holding hands with Aids patients did a tremendous amount of good in changing public attitudes. Her trip to a field of landmines became almost iconic and brought a great deal of awareness to the cause.

As the late Christopher Hitchens pointed out, the British monarchy is not wholly reliant on glamour for its survival; the long and dutiful service of Queen Elizabeth has conferred upon it a sense of obligation above personal concerns. She famously keeps her opinions to herself and the affection and esteem in which she is held by many members of the Commonwealth may be in large part down to keeping her own counsel in matters of taste and politics. Even die-hard Republicans are rarely heard criticizing the Queen and her seemingly steadfast sense of duty. Prince Philip, however, appears to find keeping his opinions to himself more difficult, which often earns him disapproval and even ridicule.

Recent polls in the UK have suggested that a majority of Britons believe their monarchy will endure for at least another 50 years and that around two thirds of those polled believed the country is better off as a monarchy than a republic. This appears to be a steady trend, as polls conducted since the 1960s have shown support for a republic remaining a minority view, despite the tremendous changes in British society during the intervening decades. Other European monarchies such as the Netherlands and Sweden also show continued support for the institution of constitutional monarchy. In most of these countries, the strength of support fluctuates, diminishing after each scandal and bolstered by milestone events such as weddings and births. Occasionally, scandals even seem to work in the royals' favour. Stories about Prince Harry's antics in Las Vegas, accompanied by some extremely candid photographs, seemed to increase his popularity among the public. Tales of infidelity, extravagant spending – particularly in times of recession – and corruption seem to inflict the most damage on the royals' public image.

It has been suggested that citizens of constitutional monarchies are happier than those of republics. Despite being less than a quarter of the world's states, they make up half of the top 30 countries appearing in the United Nations index of global well-being. Monarchies also represent seven of the top ten wealthiest countries, according to the International Monetary Fund's ranking. The British anti-monarchy campaign group Republic, however, refute claims that the institution benefits the country. They say there is no evidence it attracts tourism and claim that the Queen does indeed exercise political power. Pro-monarchists often cite the royals' ability to unite the nation but Republic query whether Britain is actually any more unified than similar republican nations. Their estimated costs to the country of £202.4 million (Republic's figure) would surely offset any perceived benefit their patronage makes to charities.

Some ousted royals have found adjustment difficult and hang on to their credentials. Constantine of Greece has been refused a Greek passport until he adopts a surname, but he nevertheless continues to use the name King Constantine instead. Simeon II of Bulgaria (a Saxe-Coburg Gotha) is the only living person to carry the title 'Tsar' as he never abdicated. He is also the only living monarch to be democratically elected as head of government following the collapse of Communist control.

There are many deposed royal hopefuls who still lay claim to their inheritances, their members littering the beaches and ski-slopes of the world, perhaps awaiting that fateful day when their devoted subjects call them back to reclaim their thrones. George Friedrich (1976–) was taken to court by two of his uncles over his claim that he was head of the House of Hohenzollern, once the rulers of Germany. He eventually won the case and told *Vanity Fair* magazine, 'The German people should think about bringing back the monarchy, I am sure it will happen.'

The following collection includes kings and queens as well as emperors, empresses, sheikhs, emirs and sultans. They are all varieties of the same breed: a state ruler who comes to power by either conquest or inheritance. Definitions can be blurred and problematic. There is a democratically elected king, queens who rule empires and many other confusions. Some aristocrats have also been included as some were of royal lines and if events had gone differently, might themselves have worn the crown.

ANCIENT
ACUMEN

The role of monarch probably first emerged many thousands of years ago. It is likely that these first kings and queens became established along with the development of agriculture, following the end of the last ice age. The early agricultural societies stayed in one place, rather than roaming in pursuit of food and they also saw an increase in their population size. Nomadic peoples tend to live in smaller groups and not all even have a chief.

As the groups of early agriculturists grew in number, their societies became increasingly complex and individuals began to specialize. In these budding cities, some members would be responsible for producing most of the food, freeing up others to concentrate on other roles, such as priest, architect or administrator. As the complexity of the communities grew, religious and military authority became increasingly centralized. It seems likely that many of the first kings also had a religious role and this combination of sacred and secular authority continues throughout history right up to the present day.

As early as the fourth millennium BCE, large population centres were being established in Ancient Egypt. There is evidence these were ruled by an elite class who embodied both religious and secular authority. A cosmetic slate, dating from around 3,000 BCE shows King Narmer performing regal duties such as smiting an unfortunate foreigner. It is generally thought to portray Narmer's unification of Upper and Lower Egypt into one kingdom but also depicts some enigmatic religious symbols.

By the end of the third millennium BCE, kingdoms and empires were rising in the Middle East. Strong leaders emerged, such as Sargon (c.2200–2145 BCE) of Akkad, often credited with being the first emperor. Legend has it that, although of lowly birth, he conquered all the neighbouring kings and founded an empire which stretched from Mesopotamia as far west as modern-day Turkey. He was a skilful military strategist and was thought to be the first leader to keep a specialized, professional army at the ready. Although he credited the gods for his victories, he promoted his warriors into an aristocratic class, funded by taxes collected from the people they conquered. He built a great library, a network of roads and even a postal system to unite his empire and facilitate its governance. His realm passed down to his sons, then a grandson and great grandson before the empire finally collapsed. For the next two thousand years, Sargon remained a model for subsequent Babylonian and Assyrian leaders.

One of the rulers to follow Sargon was Hammurabi (1696–1654 BCE), king of Babylon. He was credited with crafting one of the earliest sets of laws and they cover all aspects of Babylonian life. Known as the Code of Hammurabi, the king is identified as the final judge of all legal and social affairs. The entire code is inscribed on a stone pillar which was unearthed by archaeologists in 1901. One of the best known is 'An eye for an eye and a tooth for a tooth.' Although usually remembered as a lawgiver, Hammurabi was also an effective warrior who defeated most of his neighbours. He believed his rule was divinely sanctioned and that he was the apex of his society, towering above the three Babylonian social classes. From this majestic elevation, he endowed his kingdom with various public works such as irrigation canals, temples and fortifications.

The Mycenaeans were headed by a king and the Spartans had a dual kingship system, where two hereditary kings would rule alongside a council and an assembly. Monarchy was rare, however, among the classical era Greeks, who primarily viewed it as an antiquated form of rule fit only for those they termed 'barbarians' (such as the Persians). The Athenians famously founded the first democracy after expelling their ruling tyrants. A bitter struggle ensued between rival factions of aristocrats but eventually major reforms were instituted which enfranchised male citizens. The Romans progressed from kings and tyrants to a republic and then to emperors.

After Alexander the Great died, his empire disintegrated and much of it fell to monarchic rule. These Hellenistic rulers were hereditary and believed in divine justification and some were worshipped as living gods. The Greek philosophers developed certain theories of sovereignty which would resurface in imperial Rome and then later, during the Renaissance: that monarchy was ruled without accountability. It was justified by the king's immaculate virtues which he would express through his public beneficence.

Becoming a king or queen in ancient times was sometimes hereditary but frequently required great courage, cunning and tenacity, if only to fight off rivals from within the family. Kings were not usually just symbolic figures but often expected to lead their armies into battle and to conduct diplomatic negotiations.

An ancient royal household could be a dangerous place to live. As was the custom among the pharaohs of Egypt, Cleopatra had married her younger brother, Ptolemy XIII. At the time of their marriage, she was 18 years old and he was just ten. Although they were supposedly joint rulers, the older sister was determined to retain control. As he grew up, Ptolemy was no longer prepared to share power and entered into a struggle for supremacy with his sister. However, he was outplayed by the astute Cleopatra and overwhelmed by her Roman allies. It is thought he may eventually have drowned in the Nile.

The Romans enjoyed abundant intrigue in their struggles for power. In some cases, the instigators may have been behind the throne. One of the most notorious female figures in Roman history was Agrippina the Younger (d. 59 AD). Exiled for taking part in a conspiracy against her brother Caligula, on her return to Rome she was suspected of poisoning her husband. His death left her free to marry the Emperor Claudius, despite being his niece. She convinced him to adopt her son Nero as his own, placing him next in line to the throne and ousting Britannicus, his natural son, in the process. When Claudius died, suspicion inevitably fell on Agrippina and her poisoning ways, but Nero nevertheless succeeded his adoptive father. Because he was only 16 years old when he acceded, Agrippina took on the role of regent but as Nero grew up, her power diminished. In an attempt to regain control, she switched allegiance to Britannicus, trying to make him emperor. Nero's response was to have his adoptive brother poisoned at a banquet. Agrippina's continued meddling in Nero's dubious affairs prompted the increasingly erratic emperor to order his mother's murder, although historical accounts vary here. According to some accounts, Nero initially made three attempts to poison her. When she survived these by using antidotes, he ordered her boat to be sabotaged. The boat sank but she escaped the wreckage and swam ashore. When he heard she had survived, a furious Nero sent three assassins to conclude the task. By comparison, today's monarchy may seem a bland and bloodless bunch but it may be for the best.

More of the quotations from this section are apocryphal and of dubious provenance than in any of the other chapters; many were recorded decades, sometimes even centuries after the events.

ANCIENT ACUMEN

15

Agesilaus II, King of Sparta
(c.444–360 BCE)

Courage is of no value unless accompanied by justice. Yet if all men became just, there would be no need for courage.

· · · · · ·

When asked how far Sparta's territories stretched,
the King held forth his spear and replied:

As far as this can reach.

· · · · · ·

*If I have done any deed worthy of remembrance,
that deed will be my monument. If I have not,
no monument can preserve my memory.*

· · · · · ·

Freedom is what we reap from this way of life.

· · · · · ·

*It is not the positions that distinguish men
but men who distinguish the positions.*

· · · · · ·

When asked why Sparta had no walls, he pointed to his soldiers and said:

These are Sparta's walls.

· · · · · ·

His explanation for why Spartan swords were so short:

Because we fight close to the enemy.

· · · · · ·

Royalty consists not in vain pomp but in great virtues.

The Spartans were a notoriously militaristic bunch. Fighting was a
way of life, with seven-year-old boys removed from their families
and sent for harsh training. Martial codes pervaded every part of
Spartan society, with married men remaining in barracks until the
age of 30. Military service was compulsory and anyone thought
a coward would be shunned even by their own families.

Pyrrhus, King of Epirus
(c.318–272 BCE)

Another such victory over the Romans and we are undone.

This rueful comment came from the Hellenistic king who gave his name to victories which cost the winner more than the loser. Although he beat the Roman armies, the battles cost him heavy casualties. He was eventually killed during a night-time battle on the streets of Argos.

Claudius, Emperor of Rome
(10 BCE – AD 54)

Acquaintance lessens fame.

......

No one is free who does not lord over himself.

......

None is more miserable than he who wills everything but can do nothing.

......

Say not always what you know but always know what you say.

......

To do no evil is good, to intend no evil is better.

Akhenaten, King of Egypt
(1353–1336 BCE)

True wisdom is less presuming than folly. The wise man doubts often and changes his mind. The fool is obstinate and doubts not. He knows all things but his own ignorance.

......

To be satisfied with a little is the greatest wisdom and he that increases his riches, increases his cares; but a contented mind is a hidden treasure and trouble finds it not.

Cleopatra VII, Queen of Egypt
(69-30 BCE)

Fool! Don't you see that I could have poisoned you a hundred times had I been able to live without you?

. . . . . .

In praising Antony, I have dispraised Caesar.

. . . . . .

My honour was not yielded but merely conquered.

. . . . . .

All strange and terrible events are welcome but we despise comforts.

. . . . . .

I will not be triumphed over.

. . . . . .

Celerity is never more admired than by the negligent.

Julius Caesar, Dictator of Rome
(100-44 BCE)

Men willingly believe what they wish.

. . . . . .

Caesar's wife must be above suspicion.

. . . . . .

Better first in a village than second in Rome.

. . . . . .

I came, I saw, I conquered.

. . . . . .

The die is cast.

Caesar was said to have declared this on crossing the Rubicon.
The act of taking his army across Rome's city boundaries
made the outbreak of armed conflict inevitable.

. . . . . .

I love treason but hate a traitor.

18

Solomon, King of Israel
(c.10th century BCE)

As a man thinks in his heart, so he is.

. . . . . .

Your own soul is nourished when you are
kind; it is destroyed when you are cruel.

. . . . . .

A fool is wise in his own eyes.

. . . . . .

All the rivers run into the sea; yet the sea is not full.

. . . . . .

A good name is better than riches.

. . . . . .

Train up a child in the way that he should go and
when he is older, he will not depart from it.

. . . . . .

A merry heart is like good medicine.

. . . . . .

As iron sharpens iron, so a friend sharpens a friend.

. . . . . .

Kindness and faithfulness keep a king safe.
Through kindness his throne is made secure.

. . . . . .

In the day of prosperity be cheerful, but
in the day of adversity consider.

. . . . . .

Who is the wise man? He who sees what is going to be born.

Alexander III, Alexander the Great, Ruler of Macedon
(356–323 BCE)

I do not steal victory.

......

Remember: upon the conduct of each depends the fate of all.

......

There is nothing impossible to him who will try.

......

Sex and sleep alone make me conscious I am mortal.

......

When deliberating on a reward for one of his generals:
*I consider not what Parmenio should receive
but what Alexander should give.*

......

*I am indebted to my father for living but
to my teacher for living well.*

......

*Know ye not that the end and object of conquest is
to avoid doing the same thing as the conquered?*

Titus Flavius Vespasian, Emperor of Rome
(AD 9–79)

Money has no smell.

......

The body of a dead enemy always smells sweet.

......

It becomes an emperor to die standing.

Alexander the Great

Augustus Caesar, First Emperor of Rome
(63 BCE – AD 14)

Make haste slowly.

. . . . . .

Of Rome, Augustus said:

I found a city of brick and left it a city of marble.

. . . . . .

Better a cautious commander than a rash one.

. . . . . .

Only that which is well done is quickly done.

. . . . . .

*Young men: hear an old man to whom old
men harkened when he was young.*

Leonidas, King of Sparta
(d. 480 BCE)

When Xerxes, king of Persia demanded the Spartans hand
over their weapons, Leonidas' challenging reply was:

Come and take them.

Marcus Aurelius, Emperor of Rome
(AD 121-180)

Every instant of time is a pinprick of eternity.

. . . . . .

*Time is a violent torrent; no sooner is a thing brought to
sight than it is swept by and another takes its place.*

. . . . . .

*Nothing happens to anybody which he
is not fitted by nature to bear.*

*First, do nothing inconsiderately or without purpose; second,
act for no purpose than has no beneficial social end.*

· · · · · ·

Be in harmony with nature.

· · · · · ·

*He is poor who has need of another and has
not in himself all things useful to life.*

· · · · · ·

*Mankind was created for the sake of one another.
Therefore either instruct them, or endure them.*

· · · · · ·

*Wrong your soul and you lose the
opportunity of honouring yourself.*

· · · · · ·

*To change your mind and follow him who sets you right
is to be nonetheless the free agent that you were before.*

· · · · · ·

No man can rob us of our free will.

· · · · · ·

*How quickly things disappear; it is the
operation of nature and of the universe.*

Study not to be distracted by externals.

· · · · · ·

Your life is an expression of all your thoughts.

· · · · · ·

All is opinion.

Constantine, Emperor of Rome
(AD c.280-337)

In this sign shalt thou conquer.

The first Christian emperor was said to have adopted this motto
after seeing it written across the sky just before a battle.

. . . . . .

With free minds all are to worship their Gods.

Asboka the Great,
Emperor of the Mauryan Empire
(d.238 BCE)

*Whoever praises his own religion, due to excessive
devotion and condemns others with the thought 'Let me
glorify my own religion', only harms his own religion.
Therefore contact [between religions] is good. One should
listen to and respect the doctrines professed by others.*

. . . . . .

*All men are my children. What I desire for my own children,
and I desire their welfare and happiness both in this world
and the next, that I desire for all men. You do not understand
to what extent I desire this and if some of you do understand,
you do not understand the full extent of my desire.*

Qin Shi Huang, First Emperor of China
(259-210 BCE)

*The reason why China suffers bitterly from endless wars
is because of the existence of feudal lords and kings.*

Gaius Julius Caesar Augustus Germanicus (aka Caligula), Emperor of Rome
(AD 12-41)

Let them hate me, so long as they fear me.

. . . . . .

I wish the Roman people had but one neck!

Caligula expressed his anger when an audience's
favours ran contrary to his own at the arena.

. . . . . .

Remember that I have the right to do anything to anybody.

. . . . . .

During a feast, he suddenly burst into laughter. When asked
by two consuls why he was laughing, he replied:

*What do you suppose, except that at a single nod of mine
both of you could have your throats cut on the spot?*

. . . . . .

Caligula attempted to poison his brother but then realized he
had already taken an antidote. He reprimanded his sibling:

What? An antidote against Caesar?

Caratacus, King of the Catuvellauni
(d. c. AD 50)

On first seeing Rome:

*And can you, then, who have got such possessions
and so many of them, covet our poor huts?*

. . . . . .

The Catuvellauni were a tribe from the South East of Britain and resisted
the Roman invaders for eight years. As commonly happened, the Romans
took the defeated ruler back to Rome in chains, publicly parading him
before his execution. Caratacus bore the ordeal with such dignity and
courage that Emperor Claudius pardoned him and set him free. He was not
allowed back to England, however, and lived the rest of his life in Rome.

MEDIEVAL MONARCHS AND RENAISSANCE RULERS

Following the collapse of the Western Roman Empire, Europe experienced a period of depopulation, decentralization and uncertainty. Royal power waxed and waned as the nobility fought for overall control. Kings and emperors vied for power and the boundaries of states and nations were in a state of flux.

In England, following the arrival of William the Conqueror, castles dotted all around the country provided strongholds that could be centres of regional power and withstood the attacks of a hostile monarch. The necessity for the king to keep these noblemen on side gave rise to the system of feudalism, which became dominant throughout Europe. In return for their loyalty, noblemen were granted lands seized from others and the local peasantry provided the labour. Religious institutions were also powerful with much wealth concentrated in the various monasteries. The Normans took up positions of authority in these organizations. There would, however, be a continual vying for power between church and monarch as well as between the ruling families.

Medieval kings spent much of their time fighting: either to conquer new territories, to repel invaders or quell uprisings in their own lands. They were expected to ride into battle, as well as decide military strategy. Alliances could be forged through marriage and some of the queens proved themselves to be important players in matters of state. Margaret of Anjou was the queen consort of King Henry VI, a weak and mentally unstable ruler. She seized the opportunity for power that his deficit afforded and manoeuvred her son to be the next king. Although she was ultimately unsuccessful, she was an extremely significant figure in the battle for control between the Lancastrians and their rival Yorkists.

Superstition was rife and the monarchy was itself surrounded by numerous mystical beliefs. In France and England it was believed that victims of scrofula (a skin disease caused by tuberculosis) could be cured just by touching the king. The disease became commonly known as 'the king's evil' and hundreds would gather for grand ceremonies where the monarch would touch each sufferer. Later, this cure could be effected by proxy. Many believed they would be cured by touching a particular type of coin which the monarch had also touched. The practise continued in Britain until as late as Queen Anne at the beginning of the 18th century and even later in France, with Charles X in 1825.

Monarchs were, of course, as prone to superstitious belief as the rest of the population. James I became obsessed by the subject of sorcery and attended several witch trials. He even personally supervised the torture of some unfortunate suspects, believing witchcraft to be a dangerous threat. His fixation with the subject is thought to have inspired Shakespeare's *Macbeth*.

The idea of the divine right of kings became more prominent after medieval times. King James I even published two books on the subject, stating that royal succession should be hereditary, that the monarchy was divinely ordained and so answerable to none but God and that their subjects had no rights of resistance. Such absolutism increased resistance to his rule. It meant that the monarch held complete power to make laws and to judge others. Louis XIV of France was an absolute monarch and Charles I also favoured the idea. Had he been less absolutist, his opponents may not have resorted to regicide.

Monarchs could be despotic in their judgements and execution of the law. If the king was a direct instrument of god, then an attempt to kill him was treachery of the highest order. Would-be regicides received the most barbaric punishments, such as that of Robert-Francois Damiens, who had made a feeble attempt to kill the king of France. First, he was tortured with red-hot pincers and sulphur and had boiling liquids poured into his many wounds. Then each of his four limbs was tied to a horse and the horses sent in opposite directions, tearing his limbs from his body. His bloody torso was then burned at the stake. A huge crowd had gathered to watch the grisly spectacle, including Casanova, who remembered having to turn away several times and try to block the sound of Damiens' 'piercing shrieks'.

Traitors in England were hardly treated more kindly. Guy Fawkes and his attempt to assassinate James I in the gunpowder plot earned him the penalty of hanging, drawing and quartering: another excruciatingly cruel and slow means of despatch. By comparison, beheading royalty by sword, axe or guillotine was quick and humane.

During the Renaissance, feudalism waned as monarchs attempted to wrest power away from the nobles. Patronage of the arts became increasingly important as a signifier of a ruler's power and character. Beautiful and lavish works of art, such as illustrated manuscripts and huge tapestries were commissioned by the rich and powerful. Knowledge of the humanities was also greatly valued and the best teachers were eagerly sought for the instruction of princes. Artists such as Holbein and philosophers such as Erasmus travelled Europe, dispensing their talents to the courts. The rich would vie with each other not only to own beautiful works but also to contribute to the public good. Some of our university colleges were first donated by kings and noblemen: Henry VIII founded Trinity College, Cambridge and endowed five professorships.

The courts were the focus of local political power, cultural significance and social promotion. They attracted the brightest and best from far afield and became hotbeds of rumour, scandal and intrigue. It all revolved around the central figure of the monarch and when he or she moved to a new location, they all went along. Francis I of France, for example, was a keen huntsman and travelled all year throughout his land and at different times of year to find the best game. Estimates of the size of a French court in the 16th century vary from 8,000 to 15,000 strong, so relocating the court was a major logistical operation.

During this period, monarchs sought to consolidate and increase their control, emphasizing their Divine Right to absolute rule. On the positive side, there was greater unification and a more stable government and society but many also pushed their power too far and so the worm would soon turn.

Alfonso X, King of Castile, León and Galicia
(1221–1284)

If the Lord Almighty had consulted me before embarking upon Creation, I should have recommended something simpler.

. . . . . .

Burn old wood, read old books, drink old wines, have old friends.

. . . . . .

Those who knowingly allow the king to err, deserve the same punishment as traitors.

This Spanish king was called 'el Sabio', meaning the wise or learned. He was a scholar and travelled accompanied by many other academics.

Charlemagne, King of the Franks, King of Italy and Holy Roman Emperor
(c. 740s–814)

To have another language is to possess a second soul.

. . . . . .

Right action is better than knowledge; but in order to do what is right, we must know what is right.

. . . . . .

Charlemagne was not only a skilled military strategist but an accomplished diplomat and valued education highly. He was also a devoted father who was said to love his daughters so much that he did not allow any of them to marry while he still lived.

Edward II, King of England
(1284–1327)

Evil be to him who evil thinks.

Alfred the Great, King of Wessex
(849-899)

Remember what punishments befell us in this world when we ourselves did not cherish learning nor transmit it to other men.

......

I desired to live worthily as long as I lived and to leave after my life, to the men who should come after me, the memory of me in good works.

Alfred is still the only English monarch to be given the epithet 'the Great', earned in part by his victories against the Danes. It was while hiding from the Vikings that he reputedly burned some cakes he was supposed to be watching. He is also remembered for his legal and educational reforms, improving literacy and the understanding of Latin. He began as King of the West Saxons but many consider him to be the first king of the English.

Louis XI, King of France
(1423-1483)

He who knows not how to dissimulate, cannot reign.

Henry VIII, King of England
(1491-1547)

We are, by the sufferance of God, King of England; and the kings of England in times past never had any superior but God.

......

Rose without a thorn.

This was Henry's description of Catherine Howard, his fifth wife. He had her beheaded after only two years of marriage on a charge of treason. Her perfidious act was to marry the King despite no longer being a virgin. Henry had hastily added this new definition of treason through Parliament in order to have his way.

Henry IV, King of England
(1367-1413)

*I want there to be no peasant in my kingdom so poor
that he cannot have a chicken in his pot every Sunday.*

. . . . . .

Nations, like men, have their infancy.

. . . . . .

*The greatest art of a politician is to render
vice serviceable to the cause of virtue.*

. . . . . .

*Pride defeats its own end, by bringing the man
who seeks esteem and reverence into contempt.*

. . . . . .

*Patriotism must be founded on great principals
and supported by great virtue.*

. . . . . .

*The shortest and surest way of arriving at real knowledge
is to unlearn the lessons we have been taught, to mount
the first principles and take nobody's world about them.*

Ferdinand I, Holy Roman Emperor
(1503-1564)

His motto:
Let justice be done, though the world perish.

. . . . . .

Born in Spain, Ferdinand became emperor following Charles V's
abdication. His reign was shaped by the advances of the Ottoman
Empire and wars of religion sparked by the Protestant Reformation.

Charles V, Holy Roman Emperor
(1500–1558)

Iron hand in velvet glove.

. . . . . .

Name me an emperor who was ever struck by a cannonball.

. . . . . .

*My cousin Francis and I are in perfect
accord: he wants Milan and so do I.*

. . . . . .

*Fortune has something of the nature of a woman. If she is
too intensely wooed, she commonly goes further away.*

. . . . . .

*How absurd to try to make two men think alike on matters
of religion, when I cannot make two time-pieces agree!*

. . . . . .

*To endeavour to domineer over conscience
is to invade the citadel of heaven.*

. . . . . .

Charles spent much of his time at war: not only did he oversee
the invasions of Mexico and Peru but fought the Italian Wars,
which rumbled on for many decades. However, it was said that he
loved peace. He gradually abdicated parts of his empire and finally
retired to a monastery in Spain, where he died of malaria.

Charles IX, King of France
(1550–1574)

To an injured admiral:
The wound is yours, the pain is mine.

I SPEAK SPANISH TO GOD, ITALIAN TO WOMEN, FRENCH TO MEN AND GERMAN TO MY HORSE.

Charles V, Holy Roman Emperor
(1500–1558)

MONARCHY IN A MUDDLE

Until the 17th century, most of the world conformed to a regular arrangement: each person had their well-defined place in a hierarchical society which was topped by a monarch. This established order underwent a sea change in much of Europe during the 17th and 18th centuries. The period saw royal executions and exiles, revolution and reform and the future of monarchy looked questionable.

Although republicanism seemed to flourish first in Britain, events across the Channel during the end of the 18th century would bring about a change in the mood. France abolished their monarchy and then executed Louis XVI on the grounds of treason in 1793. A period known as the Reign of Terror saw more than 15,000 people sent to the guillotine. At the same time, France was at war with its neighbours and their economy was in free fall. Perhaps as a reaction against these alarming events, France's enemies seemed to re-establish their regard for the monarchy.

In 1649, the English beheaded King Charles I, and a period known as the Commonwealth followed but civil and political conflict continued. Finally, in 1660, a new Parliament, filled with Royalist sympathizers, restored the monarchy by inviting Charles II out of exile. His reign would last 24 years but he would be succeeded by his brother James II, who would last only three.

William of Orange was born in the Hague but descended from the unfortunate Charles I. William had married Mary, daughter of the Catholic James II, forging an Anglo-Dutch alliance against the French. It also made him a more suitable candidate for the British crown. His invasion in 1688 was therefore welcomed by the many anti-Catholic English. James II was arrested and allowed to flee to France. In an event called 'The Glorious Revolution', Parliament offered William and Mary joint command of the throne. Their royal power, however, was limited by a Bill of Rights which allotted Parliament more authority. Whilst maintaining the institution of the monarchy, the real political power had now shifted to Parliament.

William and Mary died without an heir and were succeeded by their sister-in-law Anne, the younger, Protestant daughter of James II. Her reign saw a further shift of power away from the throne, as the two-party system developed in Westminster. Anne also died without an heir and was the last of the Stuarts to reign. Parliament was once again obliged to look across the water for a Protestant successor and settled on the House of Hanover.

Although he was 52nd in line to the throne, George I was the Protestant highest on the list. His accession was threatened by various Catholic and Stuart candidates but he remained in situ. Throughout much of the 18th century, the nation's government was dominated by political, rather than royal, families. Three more Georges followed the first and William IV, dubbed Silly Billy, followed them. His short reign lasted only seven years and was beset by political crises, resulting in further erosions of royal authority. He died without any surviving children and was succeeded by his 18-year-old niece, Victoria. The future of the monarchy was again looking extremely unsteady.

Victoria was not a popular figure to begin with and the Republican movement again began to flourish. In all, she suffered seven assassination attempts but her stoic response to these dramas improved her reputation among the people. The monarchy was by now a constitutional one and although she could attempt to influence, the Queen could not command policy. As the British Empire grew, Victoria's popularity increased almost in tandem. The Empire was crucial to the revival and redesign of British royalty. As the monarchy was no longer expected to lead others into battle or to make and enforce laws, they sought other reasons for their continued existence. They found their justification in developing a symbolic value, particularly as figureheads for the rich and powerful empire. Much of the royal pageantry we now consider traditional originated during Victoria's reign. Golden and Diamond Jubilees celebrated her accession to the throne and her funeral was orchestrated as a grand public spectacle.

With Victoria's death came the end of the House of Hanover as she was succeeded by her son, Edward VII. Because of her marriage to the German Prince Albert, Edward was a Saxe-Coburg-Gotha. He waited nearly 60 years to take the role for which his whole life had been primed. He became renowned for his scandalous extra-marital affairs and enjoyment of the high life. He died only nine years after his coronation and was succeeded by his son, King George V who would ditch the old German family name for one more suitably British during World War I.

Other Imperial European powers such as Russia, Germany and Austria-Hungary abolished their monarchy after World War I. Following the Great War, they reconfigured their societies in ways that would see disastrous results for their own people and for the rest of Europe.

Charles II, King of England
(1630-1685)

I am definitely the best king in England at the moment!

. . . . . .

On Sidney Godolphin:

Never in the way and never out of the way.

Godolphin, a politician, was a favourite of Charles II
and often acted as the King's intermediary.

Napoleon Bonaparte, Napoleon I of France
(1769-1821)

*All great events hang by a hair. The man of ability takes
advantage of everything and neglects nothing that can give
him a chance of success; whilst the less able man sometimes
loses everything by neglecting a single one of those chances.*

. . . . . .

From the sublime to the ridiculous is but a step.

. . . . . .

The word 'impossible' is not French.

. . . . . .

*What is a throne? A bit of wood gilded and
covered in velvet. I am the state.*

. . . . . .

The bullet that will kill me is not yet cast.

. . . . . .

On his relationship with Josephine:

I generally had to give in.

. . . . . .

Women are nothing but machines for producing children.

Kiss the feet of Popes provided their hands are tied.

. . . . . .

I am never angry when contradicted; I seek to be enlightened.

. . . . . .

Malice delights to blacken the character of prominent men.

. . . . . .

More glorious to merit a sceptre than to possess one.

. . . . . .

He who fears being conquered is certain of defeat.

. . . . . .

Greatness is nothing unless it is lasting.

. . . . . .

Imagination governs the world.

. . . . . .

*The fool has one great advantage over a man of
sense – he is always satisfied with himself.*

. . . . . .

*Ordinarily men exercise their memory
much more than their judgement.*

. . . . . .

*There is only one favourable moment in war:
talent consists in knowing how to seize it.*

. . . . . .

*Courage cannot be counterfeited. It is the
one virtue that escapes hypocrisy.*

. . . . . .

War is becoming an anachronism.

The first emperor of France became one of the most famous European
leaders in history. His innovations revolutionized the military
and his reforms touched most aspects of French society.

A KING IS SOMETIMES OBLIGED TO COMMIT CRIMES BUT THEY ARE CRIMES OF HIS POSITION.

Napoleon Bonaparte, Napoleon I of France
(1769–1821)

Lady Mary Wortley Montagu,
(1689-1762)

*A man that is ashamed of passions that are
natural and reasonable is generally proud of
those that are shameful and silly.*

......

A face is too slight a foundation for happiness.

......

*'Tis a sort of duty to be rich, that it may be in one's
power to do good, riches being another word for power.*

......

*No entertainment is so cheap as reading nor any
pleasure so lasting. She will not want... if she
can be amused with an author in her closet.*

......

*Time has the same effect on the mind as on the face:
the predominant passion and the strongest feature
become more conspicuous from the others' retiring.*

......

*I don't say 'tis impossible for an impudent man not
to rise in the world but a moderate merit with a large
share of impudence is more probable to be advanced
than the greatest qualifications without it.*

Mary was an early feminist, a talented poet, a traveller,
eccentric and pioneer of vaccination.

William IV, King of the United Kingdom
(1765-1837)

*I have my view of things and I tell them to my ministers. If
they do not adopt them, I cannot help it. I have done my duty.*

Louis Bonaparte, King of Holland
(1778-1846)

If I wanted to do wrong, I could not.

. . . . . .

I should see an enemy of my country in anyone who would change by force that which has been established by law.

. . . . . .

Nothing need be apprehended from this miserable adventure.

Louis was one of Napoleon I's three surviving brothers and originally a soldier. His emperor brother made him king of Holland but when the two fell out, he was forced to abdicate and fled, spending most of his remaining life in Italy.

Philip Dormer Stanhope,
Earl of Chesterfield
(1694-1773)

Advice is seldom welcome; those who need it the most always want it the least.

. . . . . .

I recommend to you to take care of the minutes; for hours will take care of themselves. I am very sure that people lose two or three hours every day by not taking care of the minutes.

. . . . . .

Never seem more learned than the people you are with. Wear your learning like a pocket watch and keep it hidden. Do not pull it out to count the hours but give the time when you are asked.

. . . . . .

The scholar, without good breeding, is a pedant; the philosopher, a cynic; the soldier, a brute; and every man disagreeable.

. . . . . .

Stanhope is mainly remembered for his guide to manners called *Letters to his Son* but was also a statesman, diplomat and wit.

Frederick II, Frederick the Great of Prussia
(1712–1786)

You had better have one king than five hundred.

. . . . . .

If we are understood, more words are unnecessary; if we are not likely to be understood, they are useless.

. . . . . .

An educated people can be easily governed.

. . . . . .

A crown is merely a hat that lets the rain in.

. . . . . .

He who defends everything defends nothing.

. . . . . .

The greatest and noblest pleasure we have in this world is to discover new truths and the next is to shake off old prejudices.

. . . . . .

Diplomacy without arms is like music without instruments.

. . . . . .

All religions must be tolerated, for every man must get to heaven in his own way.

. . . . . .

Don't forget your great guns, which are the most respectable arguments of the rights of kings.

. . . . . .

If my soldiers began to think, not one of them would remain in the army.

. . . . . .

It seems to be that man is made to act rather than to know: the principles of things escape our most persevering researches.

. . . . . .

Every man has a wild beast within him.

46

I begin by taking. I shall find scholars later
to demonstrate my perfect right.

. . . . . .

Rascals! Would you live forever?
Frederick chided guards at Kolin who were hesitant to go into battle.

. . . . . .

My people and I have come to an agreement
which satisfied us both; they are to say what
they please and I am to do what I please.

. . . . . .

Religion is the idol of the mob: it adores
everything it does not understand.

. . . . . .

It has been said by a certain general, that the first object in the
establishment of an army ought to be making provision for the
belly, that being the basis and foundation of all operations.

. . . . . .

What is the good of experience if you do not reflect?

. . . . . .

They say that kings are made in the image of God.
If that is what he looks like, I feel sorry for God.

. . . . . .

I shall not survive this cruel misfortune. The consequences
will be worse than defeat itself. I have no resources left and,
to speak quite frankly, I believe everything is lost. I shall
not outlive the downfall of my country. Farewell, forever!

. . . . . .

When Austro-Hungarian forces occupied Berlin, Frederick contemplated
suicide. He was a significant Enlightenment figure as well as being a
martial success. He reformed the military, the governmental and legal
systems, encouraged religious tolerance and a rudimentary freedom of
the press. Throughout his reign, he showed a devotion to his native
Germany which made him a role model for many subsequent leaders.

Nicholas II, Tsar of Russia

George III, King of Great Britain
(1738-1820)

Born and educated in this country, I
glory in the name of Briton.

. . . . . .

Was there ever such stuff as Shakespeare? Only
one must not say so! But what think you?
What? Is there not sad stuff? What? What?

. . . . . .

Once vigorous measures appear to be the only means
left of bringing the Americans to a due submission
to the mother country, the colonies will submit.

James I, King of England
(1566-1625)

Smoking is hateful to the nose, harmful to
the brain and dangerous to the lungs.

. . . . . .

I can make a lord but only God can make a gentleman.

. . . . . .

Were I not a king, I would be a university man.

Nicholas II, Tsar of Russia
(1868-1918)

There is no justice among men.

. . . . . .

I am not ready to be tsar. I know nothing
of the business of ruling.

Nicholas was the last tsar of Russia, deposed during the Russian
Revolution and then executed, along with his family, by the Bolsheviks.

Anthony Ashley-Cooper, 3rd Earl of Shaftesbury
(1671-1713)

Truth is the most powerful thing in the world,
since even fiction itself must be governed by it
and can only please by its resemblance.

· · · · · ·

'Tis the hardest thing in the world to be a good
thinker without being a strong self-examiner.

· · · · · ·

Through certain humours or passions and from temper
merely, a man may be completely miserable, let his
outward circumstances be ever so fortunate.

· · · · · ·

A right mind and generous affection has more beauty and
charm than all other symmetries in the world besides.

· · · · · ·

Cooper was a politician and leader of the evangelical movement of
the Church of England. He introduced significant and progressive
social and industrial reforms, such as preventing women and
children under the age of ten from working in coal mines.

Charles I, King of England
(1600-1649)

Without knowledge, our life would not be worth having.

· · · · · ·

Of all losses, time is the most irrecuperable
for it can never be redeemed.

· · · · · ·

Never make a defence or an apology before you be accused.

Stanislaw I, King of Poland
(1677-1766)

To believe with certainty, we must begin with doubting.

. . . . . .

Have the courage to face a difficulty lest it
kick you harder than you bargain for.

Ludwig II, King of Bavaria
(1845-1886)

I want to remain an eternal mystery to myself and others.

. . . . . .

How can you declare me insane? After all, you
have never seen or examined me before.

. . . . . .

I can get no sense of illusion in the theatre so long
as people keep staring at me, and follow my every
expression through their opera glasses. I want to
look myself, not to be a spectacle for the masses.

. . . . . .

Ludwig's construction of elaborate, fairy-tale castles nearly bankrupt
Bavaria. To avoid further ruin, his ministers had him certified insane and
attempted to depose him. He was arrested and confined to Berg Castle
but disappeared after a walk around the grounds. His body was found the
next day, along with that of his companion. The official verdict was suicide
by drowning. However, they were both found in water which was only
waist-deep and the young Ludwig had been a strong swimmer. The autopsy
found no water in his lungs and to this day, mystery surrounds his demise.

Louis XVIII, King of France
(1755-1824)

Punctuality is the politeness of kings.

. . . . . .

A king should die on his feet.

Louis XVIII was the fourth son of King Louis XV. He fled the French
Revolution, during which most of his family were killed off and, from a safe
distance, he declared himself king. Louis promised the public a constitutional
monarchy and was welcomed following Napoleon's defeat in 1813. He
remained king until his death and was succeeded by his brother, Charles X.

Prince Otto von Bismarck,
Duke of Lauenburg
(1815-1898)

Politics is not an exact science.

. . . . . .

Politics is the art of the possible.

. . . . . .

He who has his thumb on the purse has the power.

. . . . . .

Preventative war is like committing suicide for fear of death.

. . . . . .

During the Congress of Berlin in 1878:

Europe today is a powder keg and the leaders are like
men smoking in an arsenal... A single spark will
set off an explosion that will consume us all.

Louis XIV, King of France
(1638-1715)

Has God forgotten all I have done for Him?

......

I could sooner reconcile all of Europe than two women.

......

Laws are the sovereigns of sovereigns.

......

First feelings are always the most natural.

......

*There is little that can withstand a man
who can conquer himself.*

......

*Every time I appoint someone to a vacant position, I
make a hundred people unhappy and one ungrateful.*

......

Ah, if I were not king, I should lose my temper.

Louis became king at the tender age of four and a half years old. His early years saw a French rebellion and while the fighting continued, the young king suffered many privations and even went hungry. When he came of age and assumed control, he set about ensuring his rule was absolute. He is renowned for a hawk-like approach to foreign policy. As his reign continued, his religious intolerance made him unpopular in France. Yet more unpopular was his decision to fight the War of the Spanish Succession for the sake of his grandson, Philip V. The war cost France dearly and the public turned against him.

QUICK-WITTED QUEENS

In past times, women were rarely educated to the same standards as their male counterparts and few achieved positions of power which would warrant recording their words. Queens sometimes provide an exception to this sorry inequality by being given opportunities unavailable to most women in the past. Some received an education similar to that of the princes and history, of course, was obliged to pay them attention. For this reason, they are some of the few women whose words were noted and whose lives were chronicled in detail. There are many fascinating women who, against all the odds, forged their own path in history and took control, such as Empress Wu Zetian (AD 625–705) who ruled in China; Sammu-ramat (9th century BCE) who ruled in Assyria and Amina the Nigerian queen (1560–1610).

One such example was Eleanor of Aquitaine: wife of two kings, mother of two kings and one of the most powerful women of the medieval era. She was the daughter and heir of a fabulously wealthy French nobleman who owned more land than even the king. Married at 15 to King Louis VII, of France, she quickly tired of court life and accompanied her husband on the Second Crusade to Jerusalem and Constantinople. Eleanor and her ladies reputedly wore armour and carried lances, although they did not join in the fighting. During the trip, the couple's relationship deteriorated and on their return, the marriage was annulled. Eleanor then married Henry Plantagenet who became king of England in 1154. Eleanor helped to govern his empire, which included areas of France and bore five sons and three daughters. Along with all this, she was a patron of the arts and encouraged the development of the courtly love tradition and Brittany legends. For her involvement in her sons' rebellions against their father, Eleanor was eventually captured and imprisoned. Some believe she may even have instigated one of the coups. Following Henry's death, she was released and helped her son Richard I (Richard the Lionheart) to govern, acting as his regent when he left for the Crusades. Intelligent, articulate, ambitious and beautiful, Eleanor left her mark upon the world both politically and culturally.

Elizabeth I had initially been neglected by her father, Henry VIII, in both her welfare and education. It was only when he married Catherine Parr, that Elizabeth's new stepmother set about ensuring the princess received an exemplary education. The bright young girl was a superb student and soon outshone her father in Greek and Latin. As queen, Elizabeth went on to reign for 45 years and died at the age of 70, having ruled over a nation during a time of domestic political intrigue and international conflict as well as a flourishing of the arts. Some of this fine education can perhaps be seen in the quality of her speeches (she studied oratory) and in her international diplomatic negotiations: as well as Greek and Latin, she was fluent in French and Italian.

Born in Prussia (now Poland), Catherine the Great was initially a fairly minor royal but her marriage to the German Grand Duke Peter, heir to the Russian throne, propelled her into the major league. From the start, the marriage was unhappy, although they did manage to produce one heir. Catherine was charming, intelligent and cultured, fluent in German, French and Russian. Conversely, Peter is usually portrayed as lazy, dull and mean, with an obsession for toy soldiers and military games. Certainly, the portraits of him do not depict a physically appealing man and Catherine was known to have taken lovers, including a lieutenant called Gregory Orlov. Peter became Tsar in 1762, despite being unable to speak Russian and many of his policies and reforms caused dismay among his subjects. His reign lasted only six months, when he was overthrown by a conspiracy. Catherine was almost certainly involved in the coup and may even have been the mastermind. The army swiftly swore allegiance to her and she became Empress of Russia.

Now that she was in control, unfettered by her irritating husband, Catherine was free to pursue her own policies. As an intellectual, Catherine admired the Enlightenment in Europe and embarked on a long correspondence with the period's most celebrated sceptic, Voltaire. Her epithet 'The Great' was given to her by the writer Denis Diderot, another French writer. She wanted to modernize Russia by adopting Western European ways and improving the lot of the serfs. Catherine founded a boarding school for girls of noble families and encouraged free schools to be set up, built a new theatre and sponsored many performances.

In contrast, perhaps, to her appreciation of the Enlightenment, she was also an absolutist and expansionist, increasing Russia's territories in Poland and the Crimean peninsula. In some cases, her ex-lovers were put in charge of conquered territories. She fought off several uprisings during her reign, one by a character claiming to be her missing husband Peter. She had another two children with her lover Orlov and some doubt lingered over the paternity of her first son. A powerful woman often attracts lurid rumours and history, mainly written by men, has tended to focus on Catherine's sexual appetites (including some bizarre, untrue stories). Although she did not effect the widespread reforms she might have done, she did leave Russia a significant legacy by expanding its borders and developing it culturally and educationally.

To follow are some eminent women who tussled with history, some successfully, others less so but all left their mark for posterity.

QUICK-WITTED QUEENS

Eleanor of Aquitaine, Queen consort of France and Queen consort of England
(c. 1122-1204)

Grief is not very different from illness: in the impetus of its fire it does not recognize lords, it does not fear colleagues, it does not respect or spare anyone, not even itself. Pitiful and pitied by no one, why have I come to the ignominy of this detestable old age, who was ruler of two kingdoms, mother of two kings?

Marie Antoinette, Queen of France
(1755-1793)

Let them eat cake!

This was ascribed to Marie Antoinette, who was rumoured to have said it on learning that the starving peasantry had no bread. It was almost certainly not said by her but became a useful means of showing how hopelessly out of touch the aristocracy were from the lives of ordinary people. Marie and her husband King Louis XVI were eventually executed following the French Revolution.

. . . . . .

I was a queen and you took away my crown; a wife and you killed my husband; a mother and you deprived me of my children. My blood alone remains: take it but do not make me suffer long.

. . . . . .

I have seen all, I have heard all, I have forgotten all.

. . . . . .

No one understands my ills, nor the terror that fills my breast, who does not know the heart of a mother.

. . . . . .

There is nothing new except what has been forgotten.

Mary Stuart, Queen of Scots
(1542-1587)

In my end, is my beginning.

Raised in treacherous times, Catholic Mary was imprisoned by her Protestant cousin Elizabeth I. She was the focus of several plots against Elizabeth and eventually, most reluctantly, Elizabeth signed her death warrant.

Elisabeth of Wied, Queen consort of Romania
(1843-1916)

Friendship based solely upon gratitude is like a photograph: with time it fades.

• • • • • •

Work is blessed and holy. Work is the road back again to Paradise Lost!

• • • • • •

The Republican form of government is the only rational one. I can never understand the foolish people, the fact that they continue to tolerate us.

• • • • • •

Elisabeth was an accomplished musician and singer as well as a talented painter. However, it was in the field of literature that she became better known, particularly for her traditional Romanian folk tales. She also wrote poetry, plays, novels and short stories and could write in Romanian, French and English as well as her native German. She wrote under the pen name of Carmen Sylva. Elisabeth was also unusual in that she favoured republicanism as a form of government.

Anne Boleyn, Queen consort of England
(c.1501-1536)

On Katherine of Aragon, Henry VIII's first wife:
You know, I sometimes wish that all Spaniards were at the bottom of the sea.

• • • • • •

On the miscarriage of her son:
I have miscarried of my saviour.

Mary I, Queen of England
(1516-1558)

When I am dead and opened, you shall
find Calais lying in my heart.

As her health failed during her final illness, Mary Tudor
referred to England's loss of Calais. She was also known as
Bloody Mary for her persecution of English Protestants.

. . . . . .

On seeing a portrait of her future husband, King Philip of Spain:

I am already half in love.

Christina, Queen of Sweden
(1626-1689)

Fools are more to be feared than the wicked.

. . . . . .

It is necessary to try to surpass one's self always;
this occupation ought to last as long as life.

. . . . . .

Life becomes useless and insipid when one no
longer has either friends or enemies.

Christina was admired across Europe as one of the best-educated and wittiest
women of her time. As an only child, she was given the same education
a prince would be and proved herself more than equal to the opportunity.
Her distinguished tutors were impressed by her exceptional intelligence as
well as her strong will. The renowned French philosopher Renee Descartes
taught her philosophy. She was a skilled politician and a generous patron of
the arts but her abdication in 1654 shocked the West. Uncharacteristically,
perhaps, she blamed the fact of her gender in making her unfit to carry such
onerous duties. Many suggest that it was more likely due to a reluctance to
marry or a secret conversion to Catholicism. She left Sweden and spent time
in France and Rome, befriending popes and artists. Her reputation grew and
endured for defending personal freedoms and influencing European culture.

Jane Grey, Queen of England for nine days
(1537-1554)

I ground my faith upon God's word and not upon the church.

Marie Louise, Duchess of Parma
(1791-1847)

*In a few generations more, there will probably be
no room at all allowed for animals on the earth:
no need of them, no toleration of them.*

. . . . . .

*I am convinced that our movement will be more
demoralized and weakened by blind and uncritical
admiration than by frank admission of past mistakes.*

Margrethe II, Queen of Denmark
(1940-)

*I can, of course, think what I want: just like everyone else.
I simply have to refrain from saying everything I think.*

. . . . . .

I smoke wherever there's an ashtray.

. . . . . .

*One shouldn't write one's own epitaph. I hope
people will remember me as one who did her
best and who wasn't an anachronism.*

. . . . . .

I will remain on the throne until I fall off.

. . . . . .

On first meeting her future husband:
The sky just exploded.

. . . . . .

Educated at Cambridge, the London School of Economics and the
Sorbonne, Margrethe is also a skilled painter and costume designer,
much admired by her countrymen and women. As well as her native
Danish, she speaks English, Swedish, French and German. It may
not be saying much but she has the reputation of being Europe's
most intellectual monarch. Although she stopped smoking in
public in 2006, she is apparently a chain-smoker in private.

Catherine II, Empress of Russia
(1729-1796)

I praise loudly; I blame softly.

......

I will live to make myself not feared.

......

Power without a nation's confidence is nothing.

......

I beg you take courage; the brave soul can mend even disaster.

......

I am one of the people who love the why of things.

......

*A great wind is blowing and that gives you
either imagination or a headache.*

......

*You philosophers are lucky men. You write on paper
and paper is patient. Unfortunate empress that I am,
I write on the susceptible skins of living beings.*

......

*I shall be an autocrat: that's my trade. And
the good Lord will forgive: that's his.*

......

*In my position you have to read when you want to
write and to talk when you would like to read.*

......

*Men make love more intensely at 20
but make love better at 30.*

......

*In politics, a capable ruler must be guided by
circumstances, conjectures and conjunctions.*

......

If Russians knew how to read, they would write me off.

......

I may be kindly, I am ordinarily gentle but in my line of business I am obliged to will terribly what I will at all.

......

In a letter to Voltaire:

Your wit makes others witty.

......

All this is only for the mice and myself to admire!

Catherine was commenting on her private apartments,
which she had filled with great art from around the world.
Her palace is now the State Hermitage Museum.

......

*For to tempt and to be tempted are things very
nearly allied. Whenever feeling has anything to do
in the matter, no sooner is it excited, than we have
already gone vastly farther than we are aware of.*

Mary of Teck,
Queen consort of the United Kingdom
(1867-1953)

*You are a member of the British Royal Family.
We are never tired and we all love hospitals.*

......

*There's only one thing I never did and wish
I had done: climbed over a fence.*

......

When I die, India will be found engraved on my heart.

Originally engaged to Prince Albert Victor until his early death, she
next became engaged to his brother George. Notably grand and
regal in her manner, she was Queen Elizabeth II's grandmother and
numerous hospitals, colleges and ocean liners were named after her.

Elizabeth I, Queen of England
(1533-1603)

*I do not want a husband who honours me as a
queen, if he does not love me as a woman.*

. . . . . .

A clear and innocent conscience fears nothing.

. . . . . .

*Though the sex to which I belong is considered weak, you
will nevertheless find me a rock that bends to no wind.*

. . . . . .

*Do not tell secrets to those whose faith and
silence you have not already tested.*

. . . . . .

*I may have the body of a weak and feeble woman but I have
the heart and stomach of a king and of a king of England too.*

. . . . . .

Brass shines as fair to the ignorant as gold to the goldsmiths.

. . . . . .

A fool too late bewares when all the peril is past.

. . . . . .

Those who appear the most sanctified are the worst.

. . . . . .

*To be a king and wear a crown is a thing more glorious to
them that see it than it is pleasant to them that bear it.*

. . . . . .

*I would rather be a beggar and single
than a queen and married.*

. . . . . .

*Fear not, we are of the nature of the lion and cannot
descend to the destruction of mice and such small beasts.*

One man with a head on his shoulders
is worth a dozen without.

......

God forgive you but I never can.

This was addressed to one of Elizabeth's courtiers, who had indirectly caused the death of the dashing Earl of Essex, one of Elizabeth's former favourites. Although Elizabeth initially seemed besotted by him, their relationship was a stormy one and they often argued. Essex once angrily referred to her as a 'king in petticoats' after she hit him during a dispute. The relationship soured and their estrangement escalated, with Essex finally trying to raise a rebellion against her. When this plot foundered, Essex and his co-conspirators were sent to the Tower of London and Elizabeth, reluctantly, imposed the death penalty on him. During happier times, Elizabeth had given Essex a ring with the instruction that if she should ever be angry with him, he should return it to her and she would forgive him. As he awaited his execution, Essex attempted to return this token but it fell into the hands of his enemies. Katherine, the Countess of Nottingham held on to the ring and Elizabeth, believing him too proud to ask forgiveness, signed his death warrant. On her deathbed, Katherine confessed all to the Queen, hoping for forgiveness but Elizabeth was furious and the knowledge plunged her into a period of severe depression.

......

It is a natural virtue incident to our sex to
be pitiful of those that are afflicted.

......

God has given such brave soldiers to this crown
that, if they do not frighten our neighbours, at least
they prevent us from being frightened by them.

......

I would rather go to any extreme than suffer anything
that is unworthy of my reputation, or that of my crown.

......

I have the heart of a man, not of a woman
and I am not afraid of anything.

......

My mortal foe can no ways wish me a greater harm
than England's hate: neither should death be less
welcome unto me than such a mishap betide me.

MUST! IS MUST A WORD TO BE ADDRESSED TO PRINCES? LITTLE MAN, LITTLE MAN! THY FATHER, IF HE HAD BEEN ALIVE, DURST NOT HAVE USED THAT WORD.

This was Elizabeth's admonishment to her friend and advisor, Sir Robert Cecil, who had told her she must go to bed. The Queen had spent so long agonizing over the death of the Earl of Essex, hardly eating or sleeping, that her health was deteriorating. Cecil's father William had also faithfully served the Queen.

Elizabeth I, Queen of England
(1533–1603)

Isabella I, Queen of Castile and Leon
(1451-1504)

*The distance is great from the firm belief to
the realization from concrete experience.*

Juliana, Queen of the Netherlands
(1909-2004)

It must be wonderful sport to contradict each other.

. . . . . .

*I can't understand it. I can't even understand
the people who can understand it.*

. . . . . .

*Our child will not be raised in tissue paper. We
don't even want her to hear the word 'princess'.*

. . . . . .

Peace is the biggest struggle.

. . . . . .

*You are interested in the kitchen of the world: you
want to find out what is cooking, who has a finger
in the pie and who will burn his finger.*

Beatrix, Queen of the Netherlands
(1938-)

*I realize that much will be asked of me, yet I am
resolved to accept it as a great and splendid task.*

. . . . . .

Nature is under control but not disturbed.

Anne, Queen of Great Britain
(1665-1714)

I know my own heart to be entirely English.

In her first speech to Parliament, Anne attempted to emphasize
her English identity and downplay her Dutch associations.

Marie, Queen of Romania
(1875-1938)

Fashion exists for women with no taste;
etiquette for people with no breeding.

Marguerite de Valois,
Queen of France and Navarre
(1553-1615)

A woman of honour should never suspect
another of things she would not do herself.

......

The more hidden the venom, the more dangerous it is.

......

No one perfectly loves God who does not
perfectly love some of his creatures.

......

The woman who does not choose to love should cut the
matter short at once by holding out no hopes to her suitor.

......

Tears may dry up but the heart – never!

......

It is the same in love as in war: a fortress
that parleys is half taken.

Marguerite was renowned throughout Europe for her style and beauty
but she also showed resilience and character. When her brother Henry III
imprisoned her for 18 years, she took the opportunity to write her memoirs.

Caroline of Ansbach,
Queen consort of Great Britain and Ireland
(1683-1737)

On her son, Frederick:

Our firstborn is the greatest ass, the greatest liar, the greatest canaille and the greatest beast in the world and we heartily wish he was out of it.

. . . . . .

The Prince was refused admission to his mother's chamber as she lay dying and her relieved response was:

At last I shall have one comfort in having my eyes eternally closed. I shall never have to see that monster again.

. . . . . .

Frederick, the Prince of Wales and his parents were estranged, possibly because he had long made a career of opposing them at every opportunity. Despite being the heir to the throne, he never made it to kingship as his father survived him. Avid about the new sport of cricket, Frederick was reportedly hit on the head by a cricket ball and died of a resultant abscess.

Rania Al Abdullah, Queen of Jordan
(1970-)

Being queen is overrated.

. . . . . .

At the end of the day, the position is just a position, a title is just a title and those things come and go. It's really your essence and your values that are important.

. . . . . .

Being popular comes when you have everything. But to be liked, it means that you must be treating people with respect and you must be showing kindness towards them.

. . . . . .

Religion and modernity are not necessarily mutually exclusive.

. . . . . .

I'd rather be dealt with as a person than a persona.

I found that being online has opened a window
for me to look into other people's lives. The
greatest fear that I have is losing touch.

. . . . . .

Of course democracy is good but it is
a process, not a prescription.

. . . . . .

We shouldn't judge people through the
prism of our own stereotypes.

. . . . . .

When you educate a girl, you kick-start a cycle of success.
It makes economic sense. It makes social sense. It makes
moral sense but, it seems, it's not yet common sense.

. . . . . .

To achieve lasting peace in the Middle East takes guts, not guns.

Forced to flee her native Kuwait during the first Gulf War, Rania met
Prince Abdullah II of Jordan at a party. He was not, at the time, expected
to become king but the two instantly fell for each other and were married
just six months later. She has been a rare female voice from the Arab
world and her progressive views, particularly concerning women's rights,
education and health have helped to make her an important figurehead
for the region – not at all hindered by her glamour and physical beauty.
She has also tried to challenge Western stereotypical views of the area.

Elizabeth II, Queen of the United Kingdom
(1926-)

I have to be seen to be believed.

. . . . . .

Football's a difficult business and aren't they prima donnas?

Victoria, Queen the United Kingdom
(1819-1901)

*Great events make me quiet and calm. It is
only trifles that irritate my nerves.*

· · · · · ·

*The important thing is not what they think
of me but what I think of them.*

· · · · · ·

*I would venture to warn against too great intimacy with
artists as it is very seductive and a little dangerous.*
Victoria offered this advice in a letter to one of her daughters.

· · · · · ·

*Move Queen Anne? Most certainly not! Why it
might some day be suggested that my statue should
be moved, which I should much dislike.*
Victoria was not well disposed towards the request
that a statue of Queen Anne be relocated.

· · · · · ·

*We are not interested in the possibilities
of defeat. They do not exist.*

· · · · · ·

Being pregnant is an occupational hazard of being a wife.
Victoria produced nine children.

· · · · · ·

*I don't dislike babies, though I think very
young ones rather disgusting.*

· · · · · ·

*An ugly baby is a very nasty object – and the
prettiest is frightful when undressed.*

· · · · · ·

Being married gives one one's position like nothing else can.

I think people really marry far too much. It is such a lottery after all and for a poor woman a very doubtful happiness.

· · · · · ·

A marriage is no amusement but a solemn act and generally a sad one.

· · · · · ·

I feel sure that no girl would go to the altar if she knew all.

· · · · · ·

When I think of a merry, happy, free young girl and look at the ailing, aching state a young wife generally is doomed to – which you can't deny is the penalty of marriage.

· · · · · ·

Everybody grows but me.

· · · · · ·

For a man to strike any women is most brutal and I, as well as everyone else, think this far worse than any attempt to shoot, which, wicked as it is, is at least more comprehensible and more courageous.

Victoria, who died peacefully at a considerable age, survived
several assassination attempts during her reign.

· · · · · ·

On the prime minister, William Gladstone:

He speaks to me as if I were a public meeting.

· · · · · ·

I am every day more convinced that we woman, if we are to be good women, feminine and amiable and domestic are not fitted to reign; at least it is they that drive themselves to the work which it entails.

· · · · · ·

The Queen is most anxious to enlist everyone in checking this mad, wicked folly of 'Women's Rights'. It is a subject which makes the Queen so furious that she cannot contain herself.

WE ARE NOT AMUSED!

This phrase has become synonymous with Queen Victoria and has come to epitomize the prudish veneer of Victorian society. There are various different accounts of how it first occurred, most of them relating to the Queen's displeasure at a risqué story. Sadly, there is no evidence that Victoria ever said it and the Queen herself denied having done so. Many who knew her insisted she would laugh readily. Some believe that the comment may have originated with a much earlier monarch: Queen Elizabeth I.

Victoria, Queen of the United Kingdom
(1819–1901)

THE AXEMAN COMETH... AND OTHER DYING WORDS

Although most monarchs achieve a peaceful death, the job occasionally entails the disadvantage of execution, either at the hands of revolutionaries or by a rival. Severing a monarch from their head was certainly a means of ensuring they would not return but many baulked at the notion of killing someone considered in possession of divine right. Some monarchs, however, appeared to have few qualms about killing others.

It has been estimated that somewhere between 57,000 and 72,000 subjects of Henry VIII lost their heads during his reign, which may put into perspective the handful of kings and queens who lost theirs throughout the span of history. Henry's reign may have been particularly bloody due largely to the religious conflict running through the British Isles at the time, but Henry also executed people for political and highly personal reasons. On succeeding to the throne, the King distanced himself from his unpopular father's reign by having some of the old king's advisors executed. He also had pretenders to his throne despatched, including Edmund de la Pole and Edward Stafford, both of whom had substantial claims to the throne and were descended of royal lines. Most notoriously, Henry appeared to have little compunction about killing women he had married and on the most spurious of grounds.

Anne Boleyn was convicted of adultery, incest and treason. There was no real evidence for these charges but they gave Henry public justification for ridding himself of yet another inconvenient wife. In accordance with their high status, royalty were usually beheaded. It was considered the most humane means of despatch because it was relatively quick and dignified. English executioners usually employed the axe, a tool which could sometimes be inefficient. Anne, however, was shown special favour of a sort in being killed by sword. An expert French executioner was brought from Calais specifically for the assignment; he could be relied upon to complete the task with just one blow. Reports say he reassured Anne that he would not strike until she was ready but just as he swung the blade he called out 'Where is my sword?' This was a small attempt at kindness. Anne was still at prayer, believing the executioner to be preparing himself and so the swift, precise stroke would have come unexpectedly, sparing her those last few seconds of dreadful suspense. She was the first English queen to be publicly executed.

In 1790, Doctor Joseph-Ignace Guillotin had proposed that the means of execution for every Frenchman or woman should be the same, regardless of their crime or class. In 1791, the National Assembly made the proposal law and, as was customary, the new law was co-signed by King Louis XVI. Beheading was no longer to be the preserve of a privileged few. Antoine Louis and Tobias Schmidt devised a machine which would be a modern, humane means of despatching large numbers of prisoners. In honour of the man who first proposed such a device, it was dubbed the guillotine. Thousands were put to death this way, including King Louis XVI and his wife Marie Antoinette, as well as some prominent Revolutionary figures, such as Robespierre and Danton. The guillotine's final use was in 1977 in Marseille and its use abolished in France in 1981.

If the notion of beheading being humane seems absurd then it is worth considering some of the alternatives available at the time. Treason, officially deemed the most heinous of crimes, brought the most dreadful of punishments. Male offenders would be hanged until almost dead, then cut down, castrated and disembowelled and the 'off-cuts' burned in front of them. Next, their bodies would be cut into four and finally, their head severed from what was left of their bodies. The head would usually be placed on a stake in a public place to serve as a warning. London Bridge was generally decorated in this way. Women convicted of treason would be shown some mercy by virtue of their gender and merely burned alive. For ordinary criminals, such as thieves, hanging was the more usual punishment.

Not all royal executions were as clinical as a professional or mechanical beheading, however. According to some accounts, George Plantagenet, the rebellious younger brother of Edward IV, was drowned in a vat of Malmsey, a type of fortified wine. This scene is immortalized in Shakespeare's *Richard III*, where the blame for his death is laid at Richard's feet.

It is popularly believed that Edward II (1284–1327) suffered a pointedly cruel and unusual death. Following a coup led by his wife and her lover, Edward was forced to abdicate in favour of his son, Edward III. During his subsequent imprisonment he was mocked, starved and tortured by being confined in a cell suspended over a pit of corpses. The final cruelty came when Edward was held down and a red-hot poker (or plumber's iron) pushed up through his anus, scorching his internal organs. The reasons for such an unusual murder were supposedly to leave no visible trace of the murder but also as a cruelly barbed comment on Edward's possible homosexuality. Edward's murder has since been questioned by historians and there seems to be no certainty as to how and when he finally died.

Many monarchs were killed in battle, fulfilling their kingly duties. King John of Bohemia (1296–1346) who died at the Battle of Crecy during the Hundred Years War is a notable case. The King insisted on fighting despite having gone blind a decade earlier. Richard the Lionheart died trying to quell a rebellion in France, James IV of Scotland was killed fighting the English at the battle of Flodden Field and Sverker II of Sweden died in 1210 at the battle of Gestilren.

There is another, smaller coterie of monarchs who died accidental deaths, although when a king dies in any dubious circumstances, conspiracy theories inevitably flourish. Few monarchs can have ruled without making some enemies. William II of England went hunting in the New Forest on a summer's day in AD 1100. Unfortunately for William, he became the target and his hunting expedition ended with an arrow piercing his own lung. A nobleman was later named as the culprit but the whole event is shrouded in mystery. His hunting companions panicked and left him where he fell but whether this was due to guilt or just fear of the repercussions is debatable. Some historians believe it was an assassination and others that it was simply an accident. His body was eventually found by a passing peasant.

Another king whose death was shady is that of Henry I of England (c.1068–1135), who may have died of greediness. It was said he perished from eating a surfeit of lampreys, against his physician's advice but he had been healthy right up to that point and had the inevitable collection of foes. Adolf Frederick, King of Sweden (1710–1771) was another notable glutton. He is still known in Sweden as 'the king who ate himself to death', suffering a fatal bout of indigestion after a meal of lobster, smoked herring, caviar and sauerkraut, washed down with champagne. For dessert he guzzled 14 portions of hetvägg, a sweet roll filled with creamy, sugary almond paste. There seems little doubt in his case that gluttony really was the cause of death.

There are a few other bizarre deaths which should be remembered. Martin of Aragon (1356–1410) apparently died of a bout of indigestion accompanied by uncontrollable laughter. Another merry demise was suffered by Sir Thomas Urquhart of Cromarty (1611–1660), a Scottish aristocrat who supposedly died laughing on hearing that Charles II had taken the throne. Alexander of Greece (1893–1920) was bitten by a monkey; the wounds became infected and he died of sepsis. The monkey also did not survive the encounter. Sigurd Eysteinsson (d. 892), known as Sigurd the Mighty, suffered an infection from an even more bizarre source: the severed head of his enemy. Sigurd had killed Máel Brigte the Bucktoothed in battle. Thrilled with his conquest, Sigurd seized the head and rode off with it as a trophy. However, during the ride the head's protuberant teeth scratched his leg causing an infection that killed the ferocious Viking. A contender for the most ironic death award must be Emperor Qin Shi Huang (d. 210 BC). He took several mercury pills believing they would give him eternal life: they killed him. The famous Terracotta Army were discovered in his tomb.

Considering all the potential dangers caused by rivals, revolutions and twists of fate, it is surprising so many monarchs died of natural causes but the majority did just that.

Marie Antoinette, Queen consort of France
(1755-1793)

Pardon me, sir. I did not do it on purpose.
Marie was contrite when she stepped on the
executioner's foot on her way to the guillotine.

. . . . . .

Courage? I have shown it for years. Do you think I
shall lose it at the moment my sufferings are to end?
This was Marie's response on the scaffold to the
priest who urged her to be brave.

Charles I, King of England
(1600-1649)

As he was about to be executed:

I go from a corruptible to an incorruptible crown, where
no disturbance can be, no disturbance to the world.

Anne Boleyn, Queen consort of England
(c.1501-1536)

I have heard say that the executioner is
very good, and I have a little neck.

. . . . . .

Good Christian people, I am come hither to die, for
according to the law and by the law I am judged to
die and therefore I will speak nothing against it. I am
come hither to accuse no man, nor to speak anything of
that, whereof I am accused and condemned to die.

Elizabeth I, Queen of England
(1533-1603).

All my possessions for a moment of time.
Elizabeth died of natural causes at the age of 70.

Franz Ferdinand, Archduke of Austria-Hungary

Gaius Julius Caesar Augustus Germanicus (aka Caligula), Emperor of Rome
(AD 12-41)

I live!

He was wrong. These were his last words, as assassins murdered him.

King Charles II of England
(1630-1685)

On his deathbed:

You must pardon me, gentlemen, for being an unconscionable time a-dying.

It is now thought that Charles died of uraemia, caused by kidney failure, although the suddenness of its onset did raise suspicions that he may have been poisoned.

· · · · · ·

Again on his deathbed, concerning his mistress:

Let not poor Nelly starve.

Nero, Emperor of Rome
(AD 37-68)

What an artist the world is losing in me.

The Emperor committed suicide after fleeing Rome. The Senate had declared him a public enemy when his violent and erratic behaviour finally made him too much of a liability. Nero believed he was the embodiment of the god Apollo (patron of the arts) and would give public performances of poetry and music. This was considered highly inappropriate behaviour for an emperor.

Franz Ferdinand, Archduke of Austria-Hungary
(1863-1914)

It is nothing…it is nothing.

These were the last words of the man whose assassination set off the chain of events which would eventually lead to the outbreak of World War I.

Cleopatra, Queen of Egypt
(c.69–30 BCE)

So here it is!

Famously, to avoid the indignity of Roman capture, Cleopatra committed suicide by clasping an asp to her bosom. It seems more likely, however, that she used a more sophisticated and reliable means of death. Historians now believe she may have swallowed a lethal cocktail of poisons derived from plants such as opium, hemlock and aconitum. This would have delivered her of a fast and painless death, unlike snake venom which can be painful and lingering. Her last words, as well as the means of death are not known for certain.

James Scott, Duke of Monmouth
(1649–1685)

I will make no speeches, I come to die.

. . . . . .

Pray do your business well; do not serve me as you did my Lord Russell. I have heard you struck him three or four times. If you strike me twice I cannot promise not to move... Prithee, let me feel the axe...I fear it is not sharp enough.

Scott was the eldest of Charles II's illegitimate children and had attempted to seize the throne from his uncle, James II. Despite being family, the King ordered the death penalty. Unsure of the executioner's skill, the Duke gave him six guineas to encourage good work and asked to check the blade of the axe. He was right to be concerned. After three strikes, the unfortunate Duke had still not been despatched and the executioner offered the job to anyone in the crowd who thought they could finish it. The angry mob threatened to tear him apart unless he completed the task and he took another five or more strokes of the axe before abandoning it and severing the obstinate sinews by knife. When they belatedly realized they had no portrait of the Duke, his head was sewn back on to his body and a painting hastily completed. He can be seen in London's National Portrait Gallery to this day, wearing a fine scarf about his neck. He is the last royal person to be executed in England.

Alexander the Great
(356-323 BCE)

I am dying with the help of too many physicians.

. . . . . .

When asked, on his deathbed, who should
inherit his kingdom Alexander replied:

To the strongest!

. . . . . .

The cause of Alexander's death is subject to much debate. It may have
been natural and possible causes have been suggested as liver disease,
typhoid fever, acute pancreatitis, West Nile fever or malaria, among others.
However, there is also the inevitable possibility that he was poisoned.
He was not quite 33 years old at his death and ruler of a vast empire.

King George V, King of Britain
(1865-1936)

Bugger Bognor!

This line is probably apocryphal and there are variations on the story of
how it originated. One version states it was the dying King's response
to the suggestion he visit the town again to convalesce. The physician
who attended his deathbed recorded the King's last words as 'God
damn you!' on being injected with a final (and fatal) sedative.

Vespasian, Emperor of Rome
(AD 9-79)

Woe. I think I'm becoming a god.

Many Romans believed their emperors became deified
after death. Vespasian was known for his sense of humour
and it is possible he took his leave with this joke.

MONARCHS BEHAVING BADLY

If absolute power corrupts absolutely, then it is little wonder that so many monarchs misbehaved themselves. Many could do as they liked and quite a few did just that. Add vast amounts of wealth to the mix and we have a recipe for disaster. Henry VIII had a very final way of ending a disagreement – or a marriage – which had ceased to please him. George III went potty, now thought to be the result of a disease called porphyry. Many, however, do not have the excuse of a medical condition for their poor behaviour. Some were not too bright and the common practise of royal families inter-marrying certainly narrowed the gene pool.

Many royal scandals, perhaps inevitably, concern illicit affairs. Because marriages were more often made for political rather than romantic reasons, the parties involved might have no physical attraction or sympathetic feelings towards each other. Kings were allowed – even expected – to indulge their appetites and courtesans were familiar figures in the court, many of them exercising the power and influence they earned by having the king's favour. It was estimated that Henry I (c.1069–1135) had between 20 and 25 illegitimate children from many different mistresses. Unfortunately, he had just two children by marriage and when his sole legitimate son drowned in a shipwreck, only his daughter was left to succeed him. Henry quickly re-married in an attempt to produce another male heir but their union was childless. Although the king named his daughter as rightful successor, many of the barons were unwilling to be ruled over by a woman and Henry's death led to a period of civil war.

William IV sired 10 offspring by the same woman, an actress called Dorothea Jordan. Before he became king, the two lived together for 20 years and some speculate they may secretly have married. William later married Adelaide of Saxe-Meiningen who was half his age but none of their children survived. The succession therefore passed to their niece, Princess Victoria of Kent. The British Prime Minister David Cameron is a descendant of William and Dorothea Jordan through his paternal grandmother and therefore a 5th cousin of Queen Elizabeth II.

There was a different attitude towards queens' philandering, of course, but that did not stop them from dabbling. Marie Antoinette was rumoured to have conducted an affair with a handsome Swedish soldier. They began their romance before Louis XVI became king and continued after he was crowned. Louis' impotence was common knowledge in the court and it was apparently seven years before he finally consummated their marriage. Marie and her lover lived together in her little 'pleasure house', despite the fact that it was in the grounds of Versailles. Fittingly, perhaps, the house had been built by Louis XV for his mistress Madame de Pompadour. There is no way to be sure whether any of Marie's children were fathered by the Swede but the French Revolution made the question of their paternity irrelevant.

Being born into the life of an over-privileged prince may sound idyllic but for some, the reality was far from sublime. Christian VII of Denmark (1749–1808) was clearly mentally unstable. His mother died when he was two years old and his father paid him little attention. His father remarried but his new wife disliked Christian and the old king grew more distant, descending into alcoholism and debauchery. Unsurprisingly, with such an unhappy upbringing, Christian was an anxious child and prone to panic attacks. To make matters worse, it is likely he was permanently damaged by the cruel and violent treatment handed out by his governor, who believed that beating the child would cure him of his ills. Christian later acted out this violence on others: accompanied by his gang of boys, he would roam Copenhagen, viciously stabbing passers-by with a spiked club.

By the time Christian was crowned at 17 years of age, he was already indulging his predilection for young men and prostitutes. Soon after the coronation, he married his 15-year-old cousin, Caroline Mathilda, sister of King George III of Great Britain. The unhappy young woman was isolated in the louche court as she had not been allowed to bring any of her ladies-in-waiting. Furthermore, Christian took an instant dislike to her and his stepmother did her best to make the girl's life a misery. Others suffered Christian's behaviour, too. He liked to leapfrog over the bowed backs of visiting dignitaries and slap others on the face when they spoke to him. With his favourite accomplices, he would tear through the city, smashing windows and getting into fights. So keen was he on public executions, that he would perform his own make-believe versions. He also had a rack built on which he was stretched and whipped. His physician gradually gained more influence over the increasingly unstable king and was soon dealing with matters of state, with the King readily signing whatever he was directed to. Miserable and lonely, Queen Caroline began an affair with the doctor, which she did little to conceal. Her husband seemed unconcerned by the matter but was eventually forced to sign the pair's arrest warrant by his stepmother. The doctor was executed and Caroline sent into exile. With Christian by now physically and mentally frail, his stepmother finally had the power she had long craved as she and her son ruled Denmark. Although still officially king, Christian was only to be seen at his window, pulling faces at passers-by.

Modern royalty are no more immune from questionable behaviour than their predecessors or their peers. The Spanish monarchy were restored in 1975 but have generated several scandals in that relatively short period. Princess Cristina was questioned in court over alleged money laundering and tax fraud. Both she and her husband have been at the centre of a long investigation into major corruption but having a member of the royal family cross examined in court was unprecedented. King Juan Carlos faced international censure when it was discovered that he had been hunting elephants in Botswana: not the most appropriate holiday for the president of Spain's World Wildlife Fund. The safari became public only because the King broke his hip during the trip and had to be flown home for emergency treatment. Photographs of the King posing, gun in hand, in front of a dead elephant were poorly received and he was sacked from his presidency of the conservation group. The family do not have a happy record with guns: Juan Carlos' grandson shot himself in the foot when he was 13 years old and in 1956, the King's 14-year-old brother was shot dead while they were playing together. The exact circumstances of the accident have never been completely explained. Rumours that the royal marriage is not entirely happy were compounded recently when the couple failed to celebrate their 50th wedding anniversary.

Not only European royals get themselves into trouble. The Saudi monarchy has not entirely avoided public scandal, despite being the subsidizers and regulators of their national news organizations. One of the princes was convicted of murder in 2013, although the identity of both the prince and his victim were kept secret by the authorities. The victim's father was reluctant to accept the blood money he was offered or to pardon the culprit. It has been suggested that the death penalty may therefore be exercised, which would be in keeping with the Shari 'a law practised in Saudi Arabia. Indeed, the state has often been criticized for the high number of executions it carries out (at least 47 in 2013, according to Amnesty International). However, it is extremely unusual for a member of the ruling family to receive the death penalty. Recently, scandal has even touched King Abdullah himself, with the accusation that four princesses have been imprisoned under house arrest for the past 13 years. One of the king's 20 (or so) wives has claimed that her daughters, who are now in their 30s and 40s, were locked away as punishment for unsuitable behaviour. The most notorious event was probably the 'Death of a Princess' in 1977: 19-year-old Minsha'al bint Fahd al Saud was executed for adultery following an affair with a commoner.

The British royal family have had their own litany of troubles, although they may seem trivial by comparison. Prince Harry admitted smoking marijuana, which led to the inevitable tabloid tag of 'Harry Pothead'. Princess Anne was convicted and fined for owning a dangerous dog when her pet attacked two children. In one of the lowest points so far for the family's popularity, details of Prince Charles' affair with Camilla Parker Bowles became common knowledge.

In times past, the king was commonly seen as an ideal model for his people and it may be that this notion lingers in the popular psyche. When royals behave in ways we would not like to see in ourselves, public disapproval can be immense. Perhaps the evidence of their infidelities and errors simply shows that they are human beings like the rest of us but in a rather public forum. The difficulty is when royalty put themselves above the rest of the population, playing on the notion that they are in some way superior but then show themselves to have feet of clay, just like everyone else.

George III, King of Great Britain
(1738-1820)

On America:

*Knavery seems to be so much a striking feature of
its inhabitants that it may not in the end be an evil
that they will become aliens to this kingdom.*

• • • • • •

*Lord Chancellor, did I deliver the speech well? I
am glad of that, for there was nothing in it.*

The two best remembered aspects of George III's reign are his part in the loss of
the American colonies and for his madness. His responsibility in the former may
have been overestimated and the latter was probably caused by the hereditary
blood disease porphyria. He was mentally unfit to rule for the last decade of
his reign and his eldest son took over as Prince Regent until his father's death.

George II, King of Great Britain
(1683-1760)

About General Wolf:

Mad is he? Then I hope he will bite some of my other generals.

• • • • • •

We are come for your good, for all your goods.

• • • • • •

When his dying wife urged him to remarry:

No, I shall have mistresses.

• • • • • •

George II was fascinated by military matters and was the last British
king to appear on a battlefield; at the Battle of Dettingen in 1743, where
he apparently fought with bravery. His two other passions were music
(particularly Handel) and his wife Caroline. Just as George had loathed his
own father, George I, his own son hated him and the feeling was mutual.

Thackeray described him thus, '...a choleric little sovereign; how he shook his
fist in the face of his father's courtiers; how he kicked his coat and wig about
in his rages; and called everybody thief, liar, rascal with whom he differed'.

I WISH NOTHING BUT GOOD; THEREFORE EVERYONE WHO DOES NOT AGREE WITH ME IS A TRAITOR AND A SCOUNDREL.

George III, King of Great Britain
(1738–1820)

Charles II, King of England
(1630-1685)

On Prince George of Denmark:

I have tried him drunk and I have tried him sober and there is nothing in him.

......

There are three things in life that are certain: death, taxes and that it is raining in Tavistock.

......

I always admired virtue but I could never imitate it.

Dubbed the Merry Monarch, Charles II had around 17–20 illegitimate offspring and many, many mistresses. Some of his affairs ran concurrently and he did not confine himself to the aristocracy, which was the usual practice but enjoyed the company of anyone who took his fancy. In this way, Charles showed a keen patronage of the theatre, showering expensive gifts on pretty actresses. The king officially recognized many of these illegitimate children, bestowing titles such as Duke of Richmond upon them. Charles' wife, however, bore him no children at all.

Wallis Simpson, Duchess of Windsor
(1896-1986)

Never explain, never complain.

......

You can never be too rich or too thin.

......

I look 100 and weigh 110 – you won't love me when you see the wreck England has made me.

......

I have always had the courage for the new things that life sometimes offers.

......

For a gallant spirit there can never be defeat.

I never make a trip to the United States without visiting a supermarket. To me they are more fascinating than any fashion salon.

......

I am so anxious for you not to abdicate and I think the fact that you do is going to put me in the wrong light to the entire world because they will say I could have prevented it.

......

A woman's life can really be a succession of lives, each revolving around some emotionally compelling situation or challenge and each marked off by some intense experience.

......

On Edward:

Forgive me for not writing but this man is exhausting.

......

On England:

I hate this place; I shall hate it to my grave.

......

On hearing the British were being bombed by the Nazis:

I can't say I feel sorry for them.

......

My husband gave up everything for me. I'm not a beautiful woman, I'm nothing to look at, so the only thing I can do is dress better than everyone else.

......

You have no idea how hard it is to live out a great romance.

Harry Windsor, Prince of Wales
(1984-)

I am very sorry if I caused any offence or embarrassment to anyone. It was a poor choice of costume and I apologize.
Harry had to publicly apologize after being photographed wearing a Nazi costume to a fancy dress party.

Henry VIII, King of England
(1491–1547)

There is no head, however fine, that I cannot make fly!

. . . . . .

You have sent me a Flanders mare!

On first seeing Anne of Cleeves, his fiancée, Henry flew into a rage
with Thomas Cromwell who had engineered the marriage. This may
have been the beginning of the end for Cromwell, who would end
his years of service to the King at the hands of the executioner.

. . . . . .

On the day of his wedding to Anne of Cleeves:

*My Lord, if it were not to satisfy the world and my realm, I
would not do that I must do this day for none earthly thing.*

. . . . . .

On the execution of Thomas Cromwell:

*On light pretexts, by false accusations, they made me
put to death the most faithful servant I ever had.*

Carl Gustaf XVI, King of Sweden
(1946–)

Now is the time for the King to be quiet and give no comments.

Even in the famously permissive Swedish society, some royal behaviour
has managed to elicit outrage. In 2010, revelations emerged that King Carl
Gustav had enjoyed a riotous past consisting of debauched parties and a
long affair with a pop singer. Worse still, claims surfaced that Queen Silvia's
father had Nazi connections and had profited financially from the Holocaust.
The latter claims were swiftly denied but the damage was done: subsequent
Swedish polls showed support for the monarchy at an all-time low.

Louis XIV, King of France
(1638-1715)

I am the state.
It is legal because I wish it.
I very nearly had to wait!

Louis XV, King of France
(1710-1774)

On watching his mistress's funeral cortège set off:
The marquise has a disagreeable day for her journey.

......

After me, the flood. More commonly used in its
original French form: Apres moi, le deluge.

This line has been attributed to Louis or Madame de Pompadour but may have been from neither of them. Its meaning is taken as expressing a lack of interest in what would follow once they were no longer around. Louis took little interest in state matters, preferring to concentrate on his courtesans such as Madame de Pompadour and the Comtesse du Barry. The costs of his lavish court, along with decades of war weakened the government and made more likely the revolution which came not long after his death.

Charles Windsor, Prince of Wales
(1948-)

On Chinese officials during a Royal Tour:
Appalling old waxworks.

......

Did you seriously expect me to be the first Prince
of Wales in history not to have a mistress?

This was allegedly Charles' response to Diana when she complained of his philandering with Camilla Parker Bowles.

MODERN MONARCHS

Most remaining monarchies are constitutional, which means that their sovereigns are primarily symbolic heads of state with little or no political power. There are just a handful of states still ruled by an absolute monarch, where the sovereign has supreme political control. These include Brunei, Oman, Saudi Arabia and Swaziland. In Saudi Arabia, although the king is absolute monarch, he is supposed to rule in compliance with Shari'a Law and the Qur'an. To date, Saudi Arabia remains the only Arab nation where no national elections have ever taken place and its human rights record is generally considered dismal. Bhutan moved from absolute to constitutional monarchy during the first decade of the 21st century. In Russia, absolutism continued until the Revolution. Denmark was the first European nation to introduce a constitution in 1665.

There are many different styles of modern monarchy. The Dutch royal family are well known for their more down to earth approach and it is the only republic in the world which is headed by a constitutional monarch. Queen Juliana was famously photographed riding a bicycle and was fond of a more informal approach to life, although her mother, Queen Wilhelmina was a strict authoritarian. Both Juliana and her successor, daughter Beatrix, chose their own husbands and Beatrix abdicated the throne in 2013 in favour of her son, Willem-Alexander. This followed a pattern which has become familiar for Dutch royalty: both her mother and grandmother before her also stepped aside to make way for a younger monarch. Beatrix told the Dutch people that she felt it was time to pass the responsibility on to a new generation. King Willem-Alexander appears to be continuing with an informal attitude and said that people need not address him as 'Your Majesty'. Despite this more relaxed approach, there have been riots in the Netherlands in response to royal scandals: one occurred when Beatrix married a German in 1966, another (ten years later) involved Juliana's husband and a $1.1 million (£665,000) bribe. In 1980 there were further riots after Juliana abdicated. Insurrection aside, monarchy continues to enjoy popularity in the Netherlands, where the majority are in favour of retaining it.

Many of the royal families of Europe are keen on the usual pursuits of the super-rich: hunting, holidaying and fashion. Meanwhile, scandals involving fraud and corrupt investments seem rife.

The eastern sovereigns of absolute monarchies usually hold positions of authority within their governments. The Sultan of Brunei (1946–), for example, is the also the country's Prime Minister, Finance and Defence Minister as well as the Inspector General of the Brunei Police Force.

Established during the 18th century, Swaziland's kingdom is the last absolute monarchy remaining on the continent of Africa. King Ngwenyama Mswati III (1968–) is the head of state and appoints the prime minister as well as various members of the parliament, although elections are also held every five years.

Albert II, King of Belgium
(1934-)

Belgium is modernizing itself and it gives me joy.

......

*The crisis of the 1930s and the populist reactions
of that time must not be forgotten.*

......

*But if our hopes are betrayed, if we are forced to resist
the invasion of our soil and to defend our threatened
homes, this duty, however hard it may be, will find us
armed and resolved upon the greatest sacrifices.*

......

*One single vision fills all minds: that of our independence
endangered. One single duty imposes itself upon
our wills: the duty of stubborn resistance.*

......

*In these troubled times we live in, we should remain
vigilant and see through populist arguments.*

Another member of the family previously known as Saxe-
Coburg-Gotha, Albert abdicated in 2013 in favour of his
son. He cited health reasons for stepping down.

Mohammed bin Rashid Al Maktoum,
Sheikh Mohammed,
Constitutional Monarch of Dubai
(1949-)

*My theory is that life if beautiful. Life doesn't change.
You have a day and a night and a month and a
year. We people change — we can be miserable or we
can be happy. It's what you make of your life.*

......

No one in the Emirates is above the law and accountability.

Abdullah bin Abdulaziz Al Saud, King of Saudi Arabia
(1924–)

*No matter how powerful, countries cannot rule
the whole world. The world is ruled by brains,
by justice, by morals and by fairness.*

. . . . . .

*I believe strongly in the rights of women: my
mother is a woman, my sister is a woman, my
daughter is a woman, my wife is a woman.*

Saudi Arabia has been ranked one of the five worst countries in the
world for women's rights. Women are reliant on permission from a
male guardian (usually their husband or father) before they can travel
abroad, work, attend school, have access to the law or receive medical
treatment. Women are not allowed to drive, spend time in mixed
company or choose who they will marry. It has been described as a
system of gender apartheid. King Abdullah is regarded as relatively
progressive in his views: in 2011 he declared that women will be able
to vote and run for office in the local elections to be held in 2015.

Al-Mayassa bint Hamad bin Khalifa Al-Thani, Sheikha of Qatar
(1983–)

*People have said, 'Let's build bridges' and frankly,
I want to do more than that. I would like to break
the walls of ignorance between East and West.*

. . . . . .

*In a time where the world is becoming personalized,
when the mobile phone, the burger, everything has
its own personal identity, how should we perceive
ourselves and how should we perceive others?*

The Sheikha is Chair of the Qatar Museums Authority and the Doha Film
Institute and has been described as 'the art world's most powerful woman'.

Hamad bin Khalifa Al Thani, former Emir of Qatar
(1952–)

We in the Middle East like to talk politics, we like to argue. Just look at the three prophets – Moses, Jesus and Mohammed. They are all from this small region which creates problems all the time.

......

I really don't want you to think of Qatar as a hydrocarbon country alone. We know that hydrocarbons will come and go but education will stay. It is the most important thing for us.

The Emir abdicated in 2013 in favour of his son.

Marie-Chantal Claire, Crown Princess of Greece
(1968–)

A lot of people judge me because I like to, you know, look good but I grew up in fashion.

......

I love to dress up. You have to have a sense of fun in life, too. We can all be serious and work and do our bit but every now and again you have to have a good giggle.

......

On the subject of Botox:
I would rather age gracefully than look like a monster at 60.

......

I was spending most of my summers in Greece when I was a little girl and at boarding school my first room-mate was Greek, so I guess I kind of had that Greek destiny.

Marie-Chantal is Founder and Creative Director of her own luxury children's wear brand.

Charlene, Princess of Monaco
(1978-)

Grace Kelly forged a link between Monaco and the
movie world and I would like to create a strong bond
between Monaco and the fashion community.

. . . . . .

I don't want to be a princess who sits on the sidelines; I want
to be present and actively involved. It's a life with a purpose.

. . . . . .

Some brides stress, some don't. I think I'm a serene bride.

. . . . . .

Sport has given me drive and discipline. It
also taught me to remain humble.

. . . . . .

I had been playing beach volleyball all day, painted my
nails red and threw on a green dress. I thought I looked
great at the time but looking back, I realise that my debut
into Monaco society should have been better executed!

. . . . . .

The people I mixed with in Monaco didn't relate to
my South African mentality or humour. Although
I have met some wonderful people since I've been
living in Monaco, I regard them all as acquaintances.
I only have two people I consider friends here.

. . . . . .

What's happening to our world? Imagine the year 2000
and our ozone layer has vanished... Our planet has
a fever and she is burning up – what will you do?

Charlene is a South African former Olympic swimmer
and is married to Albert II, Prince of Monaco.

Mozah bint Nasser Al Missned, Sheikha of Qatar
(1959-)

People tend to believe that to be modern you have
to disengage from your heritage but it's not true.

Mary Elizabeth Donaldson, Crown Princess of Denmark
(1972-)

Of course we have Queen Elizabeth as head of state but in
many ways we are a kind of republic. We don't have royals
in Australia so it was kind of unusual to run into those
kind of people. But aside from that it was quite ordinary.

......

I might have some Danish lessons sometime.

......

Every child at one stage dreams of being a prince or princess.

......

At 40 years old you simply know what life is about.

Hirohito, Emperor of Japan
(1901-1989)

I discovered freedom for the first time in England.

......

They do not depend upon mere legends and myths. They are
not predicated on the false conception that their emperor is
divine and that the Japanese people are superior to other races.

Hussein bin Talal, King of Jordan
(1935-1999)

I am proud of what I've done in Jordan but the region itself is sitting on a time bomb.

......

At 17, I knew the end of a dream... I would never be a schoolboy again.

......

We should face reality and our past mistakes in an honest, adult way. Boasting of glory does not make glory and singing in the dark does not dispel fear.

......

Sometimes, leaders' failures can cost these young people's lives.

Mohammed VI, King of Morocco
(1963-)

I may appear to be full of myself because I always want better.

......

As Commander of the Faithful, it is out of the question that I fight Islam. We need to fight violence and ignorance. It is true that when one strolls out one sees women with scarves and men with beards. This has always been the case in Morocco. Morocco is built on tolerance.

......

I have a lot of respect for countries where the practice of democracy is highly developed. I think, however, that each country has to have its own specific features of democracy.

......

My childhood was very sheltered. I grew up in a palace but I lived in Morocco as a Moroccan citizen.

Antoinette Gardiner and King Hussein

Hassan II, King of Morocco
(1929-1999)

*It is not cowardly, quite the contrary, to seek to meet
the adversary and know his intentions. However, it is
cowardly, shameful and treasonable to lay down arms.*

Mohammed Reza Pahlavi, Shah of Iran
(1919-1980)

*My advisors built a wall between myself and
my people. I didn't realize what was happening.
When I woke up, I had lost my people.*

......

*My main mistake was to have made an ancient
people advance by forced marches towards
independence, health, culture, affluence, comfort.*

......

Shah is a kind of magic word with the Persian people.

......

*Let me tell you quite bluntly that this king business
has given me personally nothing but headaches.*

The Shah had promised to reign constitutionally but increasingly
meddled in matters of government. He made social reforms such
as improving literacy and women's rights but in 1967 had himself
crowned 'King of Kings' and Emperor of Iran. The increasingly
repressive nature of his regime aggravated Persian liberals, who sought
democracy and religious leaders, whose authority he threatened.
His government was overthrown in 1979 and he left Iran.

Norodom Sihanouk, King of Cambodia
(1922-2012)

*Time will inevitably uncover dishonesty and
lies; history has no place for them.*

......

*Cambodia wanted no part of SEATO. We would
look after ourselves as neutrals and Buddhists.*

Sihanouk was deposed in 1970 in a coup by General Lon Nol and
supported by the United States. He returned to the throne in 1993,
following the fall of the Khmer Rouge and a Cambodian National
Assembly vote to restore the monarchy. He also served as prime
minister and president. He was a keen film-maker and composer.

Wilhelm II, King of Prussia
and the last Kaiser
(1859-1941)

Give me a woman who loves beer and I will conquer the world!

......

*I look on myself as an instrument of the Almighty and go
on my way regardless of transient opinions and views.*

......

Following Kristallnacht:

For the first time, I am ashamed to be a German.

Willem-Alexander, King of the Netherlands
(1967-)

Here in the Netherlands, there are towns that take part in the throwing of toilet bowls for a laugh.

......

I'm not a protocol fetishist. It's more important to me that people feel at ease when I'm with them.

......

People make mistakes. I will make mistakes in the future, too. I think we have learnt a lot from this and that it has also been part of the training in our preparation for kinghood.

Before becoming king, the prince had invested in a holiday-resort project which became beset by rumours of corruption. He pulled out of the project and publicly apologized on Dutch television for his involvement.

......

One has to divide attention between having kids and a full workload.

......

Sometimes it just means flying from Bogota to New York via Amsterdam to have a day with your kids. When we spend time with them, I think we do our utmost best to be really with them: on vacations or during weekends or even at breakfast in the morning.

......

I want to be a traditional king first and foremost, building on the tradition of my predecessors standing for continuity and stability in this country but also a 21st century king who can unite, represent and encourage society.

Sultan bin Abdulaziz Al Saud, Crown Prince of Saudi Arabia
(1928–2011)

We are not against religions. This country is the cradle of prophecy and the true message and we will not contradict this.

Masako, Crown Princess of Japan
(1963–)

At times I experience hardship in trying to find the proper balance between traditional things and my own personality.

Carl XVI Gustaf, King of Sweden
(1946–)

I don't like inaugurating nuclear power plants but I do it if I'm ordered to.

 . . . . . .

On absolute primogeniture:
The job is too heavy for a girl.

THE HOUSE OF WINDSOR

The dynasty which currently reigns over the United Kingdom was originally named Saxe-Coburg-Gotha. King George V changed their name by royal proclamation to the more English-sounding Windsor in 1917. His unusual action was in response to the anti-German feeling which had spread throughout Britain and the Commonwealth during World War I. Part of the name developed particularly unpleasant associations for the British, as a heavy German bomber called Gotha G.IV was brought into operation by the Imperial German Air Service.

The name of Windsor seems to have been a good choice: there was already a royal residence called Windsor Castle and the name held many other solidly British connotations. When he heard that the family name was being ditched, George V's German cousin, Emperor Wilhelm II was said to have joked that he was going to see Shakespeare's *Merry Wives of Saxe-Coburg-Gotha*.

The Windsors' reign has not always been steady. George V's rule of 26 years was followed by the coronation of his son, Edward VIII. Although he was initially a popular prince, due in part to his war service, his womanizing ways caused increasing disquiet, particularly when it became apparent that he had fallen in love with a married American woman called Wallis Simpson. Her divorce in 1936 precipitated a crisis: Edward intended to marry her but with two divorces now behind her, Wallis was not considered suitable material for a queen of the realm. Less than a year after he had been crowned king, Edward was forced to choose between the woman he loved and his sovereignty and he abdicated. He became Duke of Windsor and the couple lived abroad for the rest of their lives. Edward's younger brother Albert acceded to the throne, becoming George VI and the present queen is his daughter.

Queen Elizabeth II is the fourth monarch from the house of Windsor to be crowned and has, to date, been the longest-serving. Her coronation took place in 1952 and her reign has seen tremendous social changes take place throughout her kingdom. She is the oldest reigning British monarch and on 10 September 2015 will become the longest reigning monarch. Part of her unwavering popularity among the populace stems from the reassurance such continuity affords, along with the steadfast nature of her service to the realm. Some of the younger members of the family attract huge amounts of international attention and are global media stars.

William and Kate's wedding brought the world's press to London, endlessly picking over every detail, no matter how insignificant. Crowds of well-wishers camped out for days along the processional route, hoping for a close-up view. The birth of the royal couple's first son, Prince George, brought the media back again, with cameras avidly focused for the first appearance of the boy who may, one day, be king.

Princess Margaret, Countess of Snowdon and sister of Queen Elizabeth II
(1930-2002)

I have as much privacy as a goldfish in a bowl.

. . . . . .

When my sister and I were growing up, she was made out to be the goody-goody one.

. . . . . .

I have always had a dread of becoming a passenger in life.

. . . . . .

The Queen is the only person who can put on a tiara with one hand, while walking down stairs.

. . . . . .

I have no intention of telling people what I have for breakfast.

. . . . . .

I would like it to be known that I have decided not to marry Group Captain Peter Townsend. Mindful of the church's teaching that Christian marriage is indissoluble and conscious of my duty to the Commonwealth, I have resolved to put these considerations before any others.

Although Peter Townsend was a Battle of Britain pilot and equerry to the king, his status as a divorcee meant he was considered an unsuitable match for the princess. It was commonly believed that great pressure was put on Princess Margaret to end the romance but letters made public after her death suggest that she was unsure of whether she should marry him.

. . . . . .

Which queen are you referring to? My sister, my mother or my husband?

. . . . . .

I'm the heir apparent to the heir presumptive.

Elizabeth II, Queen of the United Kingdom
(1926-)

My husband and I...
Although rarely heard now, this phrase became so familiar in the
Queen's speeches, that it acquired the status of a catchphrase.

. . . . . .

We lost the American colonies because we lacked
the statesmanship to know the right time and the
manner of yielding what is impossible to keep.

. . . . . .

To all those who have suffered as a consequence of our troubled
past I extend my sincere thoughts and deep sympathy. With
the benefit of historical hindsight we can all see things which
we would wish had been done differently or not at all.
This was part of the Queen's speech during her first
visit to the Republic of Ireland in 2011.

. . . . . .

It's all to do with the training: you can do
a lot if you're properly trained.

. . . . . .

I declare before you all that my whole life, whether it be
long or short, shall be devoted to your service and the service
of our great imperial family to which we all belong.
From a speech made on her 21st birthday, during a tour of South Africa.

. . . . . .

Grief is the price we pay for love.

. . . . . .

The lessons from the peace process are clear: whatever
life throws at us, our individual responses will be all the
stronger for working together and sharing the load.

. . . . . .

On Margaret's children:
They are not royal, they just happen to have me as their aunt.

*I cannot lead you into battle. I do not give you laws
or administer justice but I can do something else – I
can give my heart and my devotion to these old islands
and to all the peoples of our brotherhood of nations.*

. . . . . .

*The British constitution has always been
puzzling and always will be.*

. . . . . .

*I know of no single formula for success. But over the
years I have observed that some attributes of leadership
are universal and are often about finding ways of
encouraging people to combine their efforts, talents, insights,
enthusiasm and their inspiration to work together.*

. . . . . .

*It has always been easy to hate and destroy. To
build and to cherish is much more difficult.*

. . . . . .

*1992 is not a year on which I shall look back with undiluted
pleasure. In the words of one of my more sympathetic
correspondents, it has turned out to be an 'Annus Horribilis'.*

The year had not only seen a number of royal scandals
but a disastrous fire at Windsor Castle.

. . . . . .

*Like all the best families, we have our share of eccentricities, of
impetuous and wayward youngsters and family disagreements.*

. . . . . .

I myself prefer New Zealand eggs for breakfast.

. . . . . .

These wretched babies don't come until they're ready.

. . . . . .

*For many, Christmas is also a time for coming
together. But for others, service will come first.*

*In remembering the appalling suffering of war
on both sides, we recognize how precious is the
peace we have built in Europe since 1945.*

......

*My husband has quite simply been my strength
and stay all these years and I owe him a debt
greater than he would ever claim.*

......

On meeting Eric Clapton, Jimmy Page, Jeff Beck and Brian May:
And what do you do?

......

*The upward course of a nation's history is due in the long run
to the soundness of heart of its average men and women.*

Charles Windsor, Prince of Wales
(1948-)

All the time I feel I must justify my existence.

......

*I believe passionately that everyone has
a particular God-given ability.*

......

*You have to give this much to the Luftwaffe: when it
knocked down our buildings it did not replace them with
anything more offensive than rubble. We did that.*

......

*I sometimes wonder if two thirds of the
globe is covered in red carpet.*

......

I learned the way a monkey learns: by watching its parents.

Describing the new Sainsbury Wing at the National Gallery:

*Like a monstrous carbuncle on the face of
a much-loved and elegant friend.*

· · · · · ·

On his conservation work:

*I don't want to be confronted by my future grandchild
and them say 'Why didn't you do something?'*

· · · · · ·

*I just come and talk to the plants: really very
important to talk to them, they respond, I find.*

· · · · · ·

What I want to know is: what is actually wrong with an elite?

· · · · · ·

To get the best results, you must talk to your vegetables.

· · · · · ·

On being asked whether he was in love when
announcing his engagement to Diana:

Whatever 'in love' means.

· · · · · ·

On travelling aboard the Royal Yacht:

I'd rather go by bus.

· · · · · ·

To an actress in a low-cut dress:

*Father told me that if I ever met a lady in a dress
like yours, I must look her straight in the eyes.*

· · · · · ·

I wish I were Bob Geldof.

George VI, King of the United Kingdom
(1895-1952)

The highest of distinctions is service to others.

Diana Spencer, Princess of Wales
(1961-1997)

Being a princess isn't all it's cracked up to be.

......

Family is the most important thing in the world.

......

Only do what your heart tells you.

......

*Carry out a random act of kindness, with no
expectation of reward, safe in the knowledge that
one day someone might do the same for you.*

......

*If you find someone you love in your
life, then hang on to that love.*

......

*I don't even know how to use a parking
meter, let alone a phone box.*

......

*They say it is better to be poor and happy than
rich and miserable but how about a compromise
like moderately rich and just moody?*

......

I'm thick as a plank.

......

If men had to have babies, they would only ever have one each.

......

On Prince Charles' adultery during their marriage:

There were three of us in this marriage, so it was a bit crowded.

I don't want expensive gifts; I don't want to be bought.
I have everything I want. I just want someone to be
there for me, to make me feel safe and secure.

. . . . . .

I like to be a free spirit. Some don't like
that but that's the way I am.

. . . . . .

I live for my sons. I would be lost without them.

. . . . . .

HIV does not make people dangerous to know,
so you can shake their hands and give them
a hug: Heaven knows they need it.

. . . . . .

Every one of us needs to show how much we care for
each other and, in the process, care for ourselves.

. . . . . .

Nothing brings me more happiness than trying to help the
most vulnerable people in society. Whoever is in distress
can call on me. I will come running wherever they are.

. . . . . .

When you are happy, you can forgive a great deal.

. . . . . .

On the paparazzi:
When I see them around all the time, it is like being raped.

. . . . . .

The biggest disease the world suffers from in this
day and age is that of people feeling unloved.

I'D LIKE TO BE A
QUEEN IN PEOPLE'S
HEARTS BUT I DON'T
SEE MYSELF BEING
QUEEN OF THIS
COUNTRY.

Diana Spencer, Princess of Wales
(1961–1997)

Anne, Princess Royal
(1950-)

*Golf seems to be an arduous way to go for
a walk. I prefer to take the dogs out.*

......

You are a pest, by the very nature of that camera in your hand.

......

*When I appear in public, people expect me to neigh, grind my
teeth, paw the ground and swish my tail: none of which is easy.*

......

Not bloody likely and I haven't got two million pounds!

Princess Anne's reputation as a tough, no nonsense character was enhanced
by her response to an attempted kidnapping. Her car was ambushed by
the would-be kidnapper as he fired at her bodyguards, chauffeur, a passing
policeman and a journalist following the royal party. Luckily all survived the
attempt and the culprit was apprehended and imprisoned. Anne's father,
Prince Philip is reported to have quipped: 'If the man had succeeded in
abducting Anne, she would have given him a hell of a time in captivity!'

Prince Andrew, Duke of York
(1960-)

Today is reality; yesterday is history.

......

*The Royal Family have always had an interest in a number
of different areas of society. We are a part of society.*

......

*I could have worse tags that 'Airmiles Andy'
– although I don't know what they are.*

......

*It's slightly complicated for people to grasp the
idea of a head of state in human form.*

Zara Philips, daughter of Princess Anne
(1981-)

*People still text me to say that there is something
about me in the paper and what really annoys me
is that if it's nasty, I have to go and have a look,
even though actually I don't want to know.*

. . . . . .

I don't think about the media.

. . . . . .

I hate having my picture taken.

. . . . . .

*I'm not a princess anyway so I find that
quite weird to be labelled as one.*

. . . . . .

*Virtually everything that gets printed about me is wrong
anyway so it doesn't really matter what you say.*

. . . . . .

*In our sport you're very lucky to find a horse of a
lifetime and I found mine relatively early. He's done
everything for me and I owe him the world.*

. . . . . .

*The senior members of the royal family work very
hard and I don't think people quite realize that.*

Edward VIII, King of the United Kingdom until abdication, then Duke of Windsor
(1894-1972)

I have found it impossible to carry the heavy burden of responsibility and to discharge my duties as king as I would wish to do without the help and support of the woman I love.

......

I like going there for golf. America is one vast golf course these days.

......

The thing that impresses me most about America is the way parents obey their children.

......

When you're bored with yourself, marry and be bored with someone else.

......

I wanted to be an up-to-date king but I didn't have much time.

......

Of course, I do have a slight advantage over the rest of you. It helps in a pinch to be able to remind your bride that you gave up a throne for her.

......

Perhaps one of the only positive pieces of advice that I was ever given was that supplied by an old courtier who observed: Only two rules really count: never miss an opportunity to relieve yourself and never miss a chance to sit down and rest your feet.

......

You all know the reasons which have impelled me to renounce the throne. But I want you to understand that in making up my mind I did not forget the country or the Empire which, as Prince of Wales and lately as King, I have for 25 years tried to serve.

Sarah Ferguson, Duchess of York
(1959-)

It was dreadful. They tried to put the little redhead in a cage.

. . . . . .

I felt that I ostracized myself by my behaviour, by the past, by living with all the regrets of my mistakes. That I sort of wore a hair shirt and beat myself up most of the day thinking and regretting why did I make such a mistake? Why have I made so many mistakes?

. . . . . .

I wanted to work; it's not right for a princess of the royal house to be commercial so Andrew and I decided to make the divorce official so I could go off and get a job.

. . . . . .

Diana was one of the quickest wits I knew; nobody made me laugh like her.

. . . . . .

The Queen and I always got on well, still do; I uphold everything Her Majesty represents, has given up her life for. It's her duty. For her country, she's selfless to the grave.

. . . . . .

I wish we'd never got divorced. He [Prince Andrew] and I both wish we'd never got divorced but we did. I wish I could go back and be the bride again but I can't.

George V, King of the United Kingdom
(1865-1936)

Always go to the bathroom when you have a chance.

. . . . . .

On the morning of his death:

How is the Empire?

. . . . . .

You can't shake hands with a clenched fist.

. . . . . .

On his son, Edward VIII:

After I am dead, the boy will ruin himself in 12 months.

. . . . . .

To Prince Edward VIII:

You dress like a cad; you act like a cad; you are a cad!

. . . . . .

*My father was frightened of his mother; I was
frightened of my father and I am damned well going
to see to it that my children are frightened of me.*

. . . . . .

*Is it possible that my people live in such awful conditions?
I tell you, Mr Wheatley, that if I had to live in conditions
like that, I would be a revolutionary myself.*

. . . . . .

*Today, 23 years ago, dear Grand-mamma
[Queen Victoria] died. I wonder what she would
have thought of a Labour government?*

. . . . . .

*I have many times asked myself whether there
can be more potent advocates of peace upon earth
through the years to come than this massed multitude
of silent witnesses to the desolation of war.*

After you've met 150 Lord Mayors,
they all begin to look the same.

......

To Charles Lindberg, after his solo flight across the Atlantic:

What did you do about peeing?

......

When asked why La Boheme was his favourite opera:

It's the shortest one I know.

Harry, Prince of Wales
(1984-)

There are a lot of times when myself and my brother
wish, obviously, that we were just completely normal.

......

To be honest, dinner conversations were the worst bit about
being a child and listening to the boring people around me.

......

There is no way I am going to put myself through
Sandhurst and then sit on my arse back home while
my boys are out fighting for their country.

......

On his brother, William:

It's amazing how close we've become since my mother died.
Obviously we were close but he is the one person on this earth
I can actually talk to about anything and we understand each
other and we give each other support and everything is fine.

......

Once you're in the military, she means a lot more to you
than just a grandmother. She is the Queen. And then you
suddenly start realizing, you know, wow, this is quite a big
deal. And then you get goose bumps and then the rest of it.

William, Duke of Cambridge
(1982–)

On the rise in visitors to his university town while he was studying there:
I hope I'm not a tourist attraction. I'm sure that they come here really because St Andrews is just amazing, a beautiful place.

......

I'm always open for people saying I'm wrong because most of the time I am.

......

I've had a lot of kids come up and ask for my autograph. I've had a grandmother stop me and ask me if I know a good place to buy underwear.

......

Being a small boy, it's very daunting seeing the Queen around and not really quite knowing what to talk about.

......

When the Queen says 'Well done', it means so much.

......

On doing his own shopping while a student:
The last thing I want to do is cause loads of hype or problems, I just want to go in there and get my asparagus or whatever.

Kate Middleton, Duchess of Cambridge
(1982-)

*By far the best dressing up outfit I ever had was a wonderful
pair of clown dungarees which my granny made.*

. . . . . .

On Prince William:

He's so lucky to be going out with me.

. . . . . .

*No, I had the Levi's guy on my wall,
not a picture of William, sorry.*

Kate quashed the rumours which abounded that she
had idolized William from an early age.

. . . . . .

*It's obviously nerve-wracking because I don't know
the ropes really. William is obviously used to it but
I'm willing to learn quickly and work hard.*

. . . . . .

I'm still very much Kate.

. . . . . .

*I was quite nervous about meeting William's father
but he was very, very welcoming, very friendly.
It couldn't really have gone easier for me.*

. . . . . .

I find doing speeches nerve-wracking.

Elizabeth Bowes-Lyon, Queen Mother
(1900-2002)

The children will not leave unless I do. I shall not leave unless their father does and the King will not leave the country in any circumstances whatever.

The royal family remained in London throughout World War II, even during the Blitz when the city was continually bombed by the Luftwaffe. This act of solidarity with ordinary people earned the family enormous respect and affection from many British people.

......

I'm glad we've been bombed. It makes me feel I can look the East End in the face.

......

Elizabeth had some eccentric ways of signing off her letters, such as this to a niece during the War:

Tinkety tonk, old fruit and down with the Nazis.

......

When advised not to employ gays at the palace:

We'd have to go self-service.

......

On Edwina Mountbatten being buried at sea:

Dear Edwina, she always liked a splash.

......

On the Germans:

Never trust them, never trust them. They can't be trusted.

......

Oh the Germans! If only they would choose decent leaders, then perhaps we would not need to go through the agony of war every 20 years.

......

On the French:

They are so nice and so nasty.

Elizabeth Bowes-Lyon, Queen Mother

On the first Labour government:

I am extremely anti-Labour. They are so far apart from fairies and owls and bluebells and Americans and all the things I like.

. . . . . .

Cowards falter but danger is often overcome by those who nobly dare.

. . . . . .

During a card game:

Elizabeth: How are you getting on? You don't look very happy. Lord Salisbury: Oh, Ma'am, I've been left with a horrible queen. Elizabeth: I don't think that's a very good way of putting it, do you?

. . . . . .

To Noel Coward, when she noticed him eyeing the soldiers on guard:

I wouldn't if I were you, Noel: they count them before they put them out.

. . . . . .

On the Duke of Windsor (Edward VIII):

We loved him.

. . . . . .

On Wallis Simpson:

The lowest of the low.

. . . . . .

On a visit from the poet T.S. Eliot:

We had this rather lugubrious man in a suit and he read a poem: I think it was called 'The Desert'. At first the girls got the giggles, then I did, then even the King.

On being asked what she would do with the Nebuchadnezzar
of champagne if her family didn't join her for the holidays:

I'll polish it off myself.

• • • • • •

On the title of Queen Mother:

Horrible name.

• • • • • •

In a letter to her Treasurer:

I have lost all your money at Ascot. I hope you don't mind.

• • • • • •

*I have very few friends; the people one can trust implicitly
are to be counted on the fingers of one hand.*

• • • • • •

On being widowed:

*One will never feel the same again. I talk and
laugh and listen but one's real self dies when one's
husband dies and only a ghost remains.*

• • • • • •

*Wouldn't it be terrible if you'd spent all your life doing
everything you were supposed to do: didn't drink, didn't
smoke, didn't eat things, took lots of exercise, all the things
you didn't want to do and suddenly one day you were run
over by a big red bus and as the wheels were crunching
into you you'd say 'Oh my god, I could have got so
drunk last night!' That's the way you should live your
life, as if tomorrow you'll be run over by a big red bus.*

The Queen mother died peacefully, at the age of 101.

THE PRINCE
OF GAFFES

Prince Philip, the Duke of Edinburgh, is the husband of Queen Elizabeth II and she has described him as her 'strength and stay'. To some, however, he is a short-tempered, politically incorrect blunderer but there is a far-flung corner of the world where he is worshipped as a god.

Philip was born on the island of Corfu in Greece, the product of Greek and Danish royal lines. He also claims some descent from Queen Victoria, making him a distant cousin of Queen Elizabeth II. After his uncle, King Constantine I, abdicated the Greek throne his family were banished from Greece and moved to France, Germany and Britain.

The young Philip was first educated at an American school in Paris, followed by England, Germany, then Scotland. Following graduation, he joined the Royal Naval College and saw active service in the British Navy in World War II. He took part in the Allied invasion of Sicily and was with the British Pacific fleet in the bay of Tokyo when the Japanese surrendered. Philip's sisters had married German aristocrats and Philip found himself fighting his brothers-in-law.

Philip and Elizabeth married on 20 November 1947 at Westminster Abbey in London and the ceremony was broadcast around the world by radio. The couple had first met when Philip escorted the two princesses around Dartmouth Naval College in 1939. It seems the 13-year-old Elizabeth developed a crush on the dashing cadet and the two began corresponding by letter for the next seven years. In order to marry the heir to the throne, Philip dropped his Greek and Danish titles and took British citizenship along with the name of Mountbatten. He also converted from Greek Orthodoxy to the Anglican religion.

When Elizabeth's father, King George VI died, Philip became the Queen's consort. He resigned from the Royal Navy and entered into the panoply of royal duties. Among these duties are numerous trips abroad to all corners of the world. Although Philip is not always afforded full respect at home, there is part of Vanuatu in the South Pacific where he is worshipped as a god. At some time during the 1950s or 1960s, a curious cult began to develop on the island of Tanna. A local myth told of the pale-skinned son of a mountain spirit who travelled the seas looking for a powerful woman to marry. This tale seemed to match what the islanders knew about the Queen's husband (as part of what had been an Anglo-French colony, the islanders were familiar with the royal couple) and the cult grew stronger still after they visited the islands in 1974. Philip and the islanders have exchanged gifts but they still await his return to the island, where they promise they will build him a house and he will have many wives. They say the Queen can come too, if she likes.

During his leisure time, Philip enjoys activities including flying, sailing, playing polo, carriage racing and shooting, although he has had to abandon some of these activities due to his advancing years. Irascible and outspoken, his utterances induce a mixture of horror and hilarity from Britain's subjects. His 90th birthday gave many newspaper editors (never one of Philip's favourite species) the opportunity to revisit some of his most celebrated gaffes. *The Independent* even ran '90 gaffes for 90 years' but they had some personal experience of Philip's charm, as we shall see.

Philip, Duke of Edinburgh, husband to Queen Elizabeth II
(1921-)

∞∞∞∞∞∞∞∞∞ **A Man of the World** ∞∞∞∞∞∞∞∞∞

We don't come to Canada for our health. We can think of other ways of enjoying ourselves.

· · · · · ·

To a British tourist in Papua, New Guinea:
You've managed not to get eaten, then?

· · · · · ·

To the dictator of Paraguay:
It's a pleasure to be in a country that isn't ruled by its people.

· · · · · ·

To the President of Nigeria, attired in his national dress:
You look like you're ready for bed!

· · · · · ·

To a tourist in Hungary:
You can't have been here that long, you don't have a pot belly!

· · · · · ·

To an Aboriginal leader in Queensland, Australia:
Do you still throw spears at each other?

· · · · · ·

Whilst accepting a conservation award in Thailand:
Your country is one of the most notorious centres of trading in endangered species.

· · · · · ·

Reichskanzler
Philip addressed the German Chancellor Helmut Kohl using Hitler's title.

· · · · · ·

To Cayman Islanders:
Aren't most of you descended from pirates?

LOCAL VIP: *How was your flight, sir?*
PHILIP: *Have you ever been in a plane?*
VIP: *Oh, yes sir!*
PHILIP: *Well it was like that!*

• • • • • •

I'd like to go to Russia very much – although the bastards murdered half my family!

• • • • • •

On being asked whether the Queen was enjoying her trip to Paris:
Damn fool question!

• • • • • •

To a British student in China:
If you stay here much longer, you'll go home with slitty eyes.

• • • • • •

His verdict on Beijing:
Ghastly.

∞∞∞ Philip on Britain and the British ∞∞∞

His assessment of Stoke On Trent:
Ghastly.

• • • • • •

To a Scottish driving instructor:
How do you keep the natives off the booze long enough to pass the test?

• • • • • •

At a youth club for British Bangladeshis:
So who's on drugs here? HE looks like he's on drugs!

• • • • • •

In a speech when made Chancellor of Edinburgh University:
Only a Scotsman can really survive a Scottish education.

• • • • • •

To deaf children standing near a steel band:
Deaf? If you're standing near there, no wonder you're deaf!

To black Conservative politician Lord Taylor of Warwick:

And what exotic part of the world do you come from?

. . . . . .

*Young people are the same as they
always were: just as ignorant.*

. . . . . .

On seeing some dodgy wiring at a Scottish factory:

It looks like it was put in by an Indian!

Philip later back-tracked, saying he had meant to say 'a cowboy'.

. . . . . .

On the recession:

*A few years ago, everybody was saying we must have more
leisure, everyone's working too much. Now everybody's got
more leisure time they're complaining they're unemployed.
People don't seem to make up their minds what they want.*

. . . . . .

To the republican editor of the Independent:

PHILIP: *What are you doing here?*
EDITOR: *You invited me, sir.*
PHILIP: *Well, you didn't have to come!*

. . . . . .

When asked whether he knew of the Scilly Isles:

My son…er…owns them.

. . . . . .

*The problem with London is the tourists.
They cause the congestion.*

∞∞∞∞∞∞∞∞∞∞∞∞ **Prince Charming** ∞∞∞∞∞∞∞∞∞∞∞∞

*When a man opens a car door for his wife,
it's either a new car or a new wife.*

. . . . . .

*I don't think a prostitute is more moral than a
wife but they are doing the same thing.*

Queen Elizabeth II and Prince Philip, Duke of Edinburgh walk past Elton John

During a performance by Elton John:

I wish he'd turn the microphone off.

. . . . . .

To a female sea cadet:

Do you work in a strip club?

. . . . . .

People think there's a rigid class system here but dukes have been known to marry chorus girls. Some have even married Americans.

. . . . . .

To the chairman of Channel 4:

So you're responsible for the kind of crap Channel 4 produces!

. . . . . .

When introduced to a female solicitor:

I thought it was against the law for a woman to solicit.

. . . . . .

On being told Madonna was about to sing:

Do we need earplugs?

. . . . . .

To a female politician wearing a tartan tie:

That's a nice tie; do you have any knickers in the same material?

. . . . . .

On being introduced to the actor Cate Blanchett and told she worked in the film industry:

Well, can you fix my DVD player, then? There's a cord sticking out of the back; might you tell me where it goes?

. . . . . .

To the resident of a nursing home in a wheelchair:

Do they trip over you?

. . . . . .

To a blind woman with her guide dog:

You know they have eating dogs now for anorexics?

To a female journalist at a World Wildlife Fund gala:

You're not wearing mink knickers, are you?

• • • • • •

To an elderly man who had failed to recognize him:

You bloody silly fool!

• • • • • •

On Tom Jones:

*How does one get immensely valuable by
singing the most hideous songs?*

• • • • • •

On the difficulty of getting rich in Britain:

*What about Tom Jones? He's made a million
and he's a bloody awful singer!*

• • • • • •

On meeting Tom Jones after a performance:

What do you gargle with? Pebbles?

• • • • • •

To a 13-year-old boy who wanted to be an astronaut:

You'll need to lose some weight.

◇◇◇◇◇◇◇◇ **The Way to a Man's Heart...** ◇◇◇◇◇◇◇◇

I never see any home cooking − all I get is fancy stuff.

• • • • • •

On being offered the finest Italian wines at a state banquet in Rome:

Get me a beer. I don't care what sort, just get me a beer!

• • • • • •

When presented with a hamper of goods by the US ambassador:

Where's the Southern Comfort?

• • • • • •

The French don't know how to cook breakfast.

• • • • • •

British women can't cook.

• • • • • •

Bugger the table plan − give me my dinner!

⸮⸮⸮ **Philip on Philip...and his family** ⸮⸮⸮

*I've never been noticeably reticent about talking
on subjects about which I know nothing.*

......

*Dontopedalogy is the science of opening your mouth and
putting your foot in it, which I've practised for many years.*

......

On his official duties:

*Any bloody fool can lay a wreath at the thingummy.
I'd much rather have stayed in the Navy, frankly.*

......

*It's my custom to say something flattering to begin with
so I'm excused when I put my foot in it later on.*

......

On the royal family's financial situation:

*If we go into the red next year. I shall
probably have to give up polo.*

......

On his daughter, Princess Anne:

If it doesn't fart or eat hay, she isn't interested.

......

On his son, Prince Andrew's new home:

It looks like a tart's bedroom.

......

On Buckingham Palace:

*We live in what virtually amounts to a museum...
which doesn't happen to a lot of people.*

......

Constitutionally, I don't exist.

......

*You can take it from me that the Queen has
the quality of tolerance in abundance.*

Thomas More parts from his daughter before his execution

THE REST ON ROYALTY

Everyone is familiar with the idea of royalty. Even if we live in a republic, most of us grow up with fairy tales about princesses locked in towers and handsome princes who set out on quests. Our history books are full of stories of the men and women who helped shape our nations' histories. Many contemporary monarchs are as familiar to us as soap stars and often seem to fulfil a similar role, as the press avidly follow their every scandal and mis-step as well as their weddings, births and deaths. It stands to reason, then, that most of us hold an opinion on the institution and the individuals who represent it and these opinions can be fierce and forthright. A selection of some of these varied views follow: some positive, some hostile, some thoughtful and some mischievous.

THE REST ON ROYALTY

We have a pretty witty king
Whose word no man relies on;
He never said a foolish thing,
Nor ever did a wise one.

John Wilmot, 2ⁿᵈ Earl of Rochester and poet (1647–1680) – speaking about Charles II.

It was rumoured that when the king saw this ditty, he commented, 'This is very true, for my words are my own and my actions are my ministers.'

......

One man to live in pleasure and wealth while all others weep and smart for it, that is the part not of a king but of a jailer.

Thomas More, philosopher (1478–1535)

......

There's a fine line between gossip and history,
when one is talking about kings.

Michelle Cooper, writer (1969–)

......

The silence of the people is a warning for the king.

French proverb

......

I was only saying to the Queen the other
day how I hate name-dropping.

Douglas Fairbanks, Jr, actor (1909–2000)

......

What are kings, when regiment is gone,
But perfect shadows in a sunshine day?

From Edward the Second by Christopher Marlowe (c.1564 –1593)

......

I wouldn't let that family near me with
a sharp stick, let alone a sword.

Keith Richards, musician (1943 –)

......

When asked if he would accept a knighthood:

It is better to be without a king than to have a bad one.

Chanakya, philosopher (370–283 BC)

There's no royalty in America, so people deify actors.
Joseph Gordon Levitt, actor (1981–)

......

Everyone likes flattery and when it comes to
royalty, you should lay it on with a trowel.
Benjamin Disraeli, British prime minister (1804–1881)

......

When you look at Prince Charles, don't you
think that someone in the Royal Family
knew someone in the Royal Family?
Robin Williams, actor (1951–)

......

There is no necessity to separate the monarch
from the mob; all authority is equally bad.
Oscar Wilde, writer (1854–1900)

......

Vulgarity in a king flatters the majority of the nation.
∞
Kings are not born: they are made by universal hallucination.
George Bernard Shaw, playwright (1856–1950)

......

Majesty and love do not consort well together,
nor do they dwell in the same place.
Ovid, writer (43 BC–AD 17/18)

......

If I could dress anyone, I'd like to dress the Queen, she can
handle anything. I'd put her in black – she never wears black
– and add a little leather, maybe: a little rock and roll.
Donatella Versace, designer (1955–)

......

The institution of royalty in any form
is an insult to the human race.
Mark Twain, writer (1835–1910)

*A monarch, when good, is entitled to the consideration
which we accord to a pirate who keeps Sunday school
between crimes; when bad, he is entitled to none at all.*
Mark Twain, writer (1835–1910)

. . . . . .

*I have nothing against the Queen of England. Even in
my heart I never resented her for not being Jackie Kennedy.
She is, to my mind, a very gallant lady, victimized by
whoever it is who designs the tops of her uniforms.*
Leonard Cohen, musician (1934–)

. . . . . .

*Once you touch the trappings of monarchy, like opening
an Egyptian tomb, the inside is liable to crumble.*
Anthony Sampson, writer (1926–2004)

. . . . . .

*The best reason why Monarchy is a strong government is that it
is an intelligible government. The mass of mankind understands
it and they hardly anywhere in the world understand any other.*
Walter Bagehot, economist and journalist (1826–1877)

. . . . . .

*Men will never be free until the last king is
strangled with the entrails of the last priest.*
Denis Diderot, philosopher (1713–1784)

. . . . . .

*Every noble crown is and on earth will
forever be, a crown of thorns.*
Thomas Carlyle, philosopher (1795–1881)

. . . . . .

The first art to be learned by a ruler is to endure envy.
Seneca, philosopher (4 BC–AD 65)

. . . . . .

Many a crown covers bald foreheads.
Elizabeth Barrett Browning, poet (1806–1861)

Princes are like heavenly bodies, which cause good or evil times and which have much veneration but no rest.
Francis Bacon, philosopher (1561–1626)

......

A man's a man,
But when you see a king,
You see the work
Of many thousand men.
George Eliot, writer (1819–1880)

......

Whenever monarchs err, the people are punished.
∞
Keep clear of courts: a homely life transcends
The vaunted bliss of monarchs and their friends.
Horace, poet (65–8 BC)

......

They say princes learn no art truly but the art of horsemanship. The reason is, the brave beast is no flatterer. He will throw a prince as soon as his groom.
∞
A prince without letters is a pilot without eyes. All his government is groping.
Ben Jonson, writer (1572–1637)

......

Being born into the Royal Family is like being born into a mental asylum. Marrying into it is not something to be taken lightly.
John Lydon, musician (1956–)

......

Princes give me sufficiently if they take nothing from me and do me much good if they do me no hurt; it is all I require of them.
Michel de Montaigne, writer (1533–1592)

BEING BORN INTO
THE ROYAL FAMILY IS
LIKE BEING BORN INTO
A MENTAL ASYLUM.
MARRYING INTO IT IS
NOT SOMETHING TO BE
TAKEN LIGHTLY.

John Lydon, musician
(1956–)

The king goes as far as he may, not as far as he could.
Spanish proverb

......

I don't think the so-called royal family speak for England now and I don't think England needs them. I do seriously believe that they are benefit scroungers, nothing else. I don't believe they serve any purpose whatsoever.
Steven Patrick Morrissey, musician (1959–)

......

There is something behind the throne greater than the king himself.
William Pitt the Elder, politician (1708–1778)

......

If your job is to leaven ordinary lives with elevating spectacle, be elevating or be gone.
George F. Will, writer (1941–)

......

I couldn't be royal. It's like living in a supersonic goldfish bowl.
Ozzy Osbourne, musician (1948–)

......

Divine right of kings means the divine right of anyone who can get uppermost.
Herbert Spencer, philosopher (1820–1903)

......

Monarchists frequently declare that without the royal family, Britain would be 'nothing'. What a woeful lack of love for one's country such statements express.
Julie Burchill, writer (1959–)

......

If you shoot at a king you must kill him.
Ralph Waldo Emerson, writer (1803–1882)

Commenting on the wedding of William and Kate:

I am a staunch republican but I was up at 8 a.m. in front of the telly, still in my nightie but wearing a plastic tiara... And you wondered if the ecstatic response of the crowds to glimpses of the royal family sweeping past was really about the magic of royalty or whether it was a response to their undoubted celebrity... Globalized media make the British royal family everyone's property.

Diane Abbot, Member of Parliament (1953–)

• • • • • •

I believe the people should be sovereign in Parliament, not the Crown. That magnificent gold throne in the House of Lords would look lovely in a museum. Once that happens, I don't have a problem with having a monarchy that is symbolic... [The Queen] does her job pretty well, playing the role of our national figurehead with diligence and decorum, giving us a sense of continuity in a world where change seems to be getting faster. My respect for our monarch is entirely personal – it is not vested in her office.

Billy Bragg, musician (1957–)

• • • • • •

The monarchy makes fools of us. It demands and receives deference for reasons of birth.

Michael Rosen, writer (1946–)

• • • • • •

The greatest slave in a kingdom is generally the king of it.

Sir Fulke Greville, 1st Baron Brooke (1554–1628)

• • • • • •

Monarchy remains... our keeper of continuity, anchoring us to a historical identity impervious to the next Windows upgrade; and that in an age when much that was culturally familiar has gone, been disconnected, or usurped for profit.

DBC Pierre, writer (1961–)

The royal family has very little impact now. They contribute a sense of background continuity simply by being there, and that reassures many people. But what is really dynamic and important in today's world passes them by.
Joan Bakewell, broadcaster (1933–)

. . . . . .

Kings are the slaves of history.
Leo Tolstoy, writer (1828–1910) from *War and Peace*.

. . . . . .

I always believe the rule by king or official leader is outdated. Now we must catch up with the modern world.
Dalai Lama, religious leader (1935–)

. . . . . .

There is no king who has not had a slave among his ancestors and no slave who has not had a king among his.
Hellen Keller, writer and campaigner (1880–1968)

. . . . . .

The monarchy is the representative of a society still riven with class inequalities and the need to position oneself, always. The monarchy creates insecurities in all, of whatever background.
Susie Orbach, psychotherapist (1946–)

. . . . . .

There is something exceedingly ridiculous in the composition of monarch. One of the strongest natural proofs of the folly of the hereditary rights in kings is, that nature disapproves it; otherwise she would not so frequently turn it into ridicule by giving mankind an ass for a lion.
Thomas Paine, political theorist (1737–1809)

. . . . . .

Too many kings can ruin an army.
Homer, writer (c. 8th century BC)

*I think the monarchy has become a sort of beloved national
soap opera, along the lines of an ermine-trimmed Corrie but
a bit more expensive to run… But it gets a bit repetitive and
it can't be very nice for the actors, who are stuck in roles they
can't escape from. Maybe it's time to draw the series to a close.*
Marina Lewycka, novelist (1946–)

• • • • • •

When asked her opinion of the monarchy:
Blooming marvellous, and why not.
Camila Batmanghelidjh, charity leader (1963–)

• • • • • •

Being happy is better than being king.
African proverb

• • • • • •

*I used to think [the monarchy] were completely useless
and we should get rid of them. I don't necessarily
feel that way anymore. I'm still ambivalent; I still
loathe the British class system and the royal family
are the apex of the British class system.*
Dame Helen Mirren, actor (1945–)

• • • • • •

Commenting on the birth of Edward VIII:
*From his childhood onwards, this boy will be surrounded
by sycophants and flatterers. In due course, following the
precedent which has already been set, he will be sent on
a tour of the world and probably rumour of a morganatic
marriage alliance will follow and the end of it all will be
that the country will be called upon to pay the bill.*
James Keir Hardie, politician (1856–1915)

• • • • • •

*There are many reasons for the decline in royal esteem.
One is that so many of the royals are thick.*
Alistair Campbell, journalist (1957–)

×××××××××××× **William Shakespeare** ××××××××××××
poet and playwright (c.1564–1616)

Not all the water in the rough rude sea
Can wash the balm from an anointed king
Richard II, Act III, Scene II

. . . . . .

Uneasy lies the head that wears a crown.
Henry IV, Part 2, Act III, Scene I

. . . . . .

My crown is in my heart, not on my head;
Not deck'd with diamonds and Indian stones,
Nor to be seen: my crown is call'd content,
A crown it is that seldom kings enjoy
Henry VI, Part 3, Act III Scene I

. . . . . .

What infinite heart's-ease
Must kings neglect, that private men enjoy!
And what have kings, that privates have not too,
Save ceremony, save general ceremony?
Henry V , Act IV, Scene I